# HOW GOD DID IT — NOT WHY

# How God Did It

## Not Why

William Lowell Putnam III

Light Technology Publishing

For more information about special discounts for bulk purchases, please contact Lowell Observatory, Mount Washington Observatory (see Preface for details), or Light Technology Publishing.

ISBN-13: 978-1-62233-015-7
Published and printed in the United States of America by:

Light Technology Publishing

PO Box 3540
Flagstaff, AZ 86003
800-450-0985
www.LightTechnology.com

# Contents

Take a last look! With global warming and consequent sea level rise, oceanic islands such as Fiji, shown here in a photo from 2000, will get vastly smaller. Lagoons, such as this one, will become deeper, more oceanic, and seriously alter the lives and livelihoods of all such islanders. This book, the climax of my literary career, is dedicated to the lady in the foreground, my late spouse Kathryn, whose love, patience, and wisdom guided my life for sixty-three years.

— *William L. Putnam III*

# Preface

## Warning!

What follows is not a work of religion, philosophy, or science. Though it may appear to contain a few matters worthy of argument, it is intended (except for the penultimate chapter) to be simply a collection of fact — pertinent to the planet all of God's creatures live on. If that is not what you are after, then you should look elsewhere.

Although there is only one scribe — undersigned — this opus represents, in great part, the cumulative effort of a number of longtime fact finders, many of whom are associated with Percival Lowell's Observatory in Flagstaff, Arizona, and named in the forthcoming Acknowledgments rather than in the location where each contributor's more specific contributions are to be found. The goal of this work is to place a great many simple, historic, and well-known facts in appropriate context with the environmental issues facing planet Earth and humanity in the early twenty-first century of the Christian Era and after some five or more billion earthly circuits around the medium-sized parent star that humanity calls the Sun.

It is the hope of the undersigned that, in order to give the unfortunate purchaser some semblance of his or her money's worth, the many pictures of the declining state of health of planet Earth that illustrate this opus will provide 1,000 words apiece of factual value.

THIS BOOK IS PUBLISHED JOINTLY FOR:

**The Lowell Observatory** *(home of the expanding universe)*
1400 W. Mars Hill Rd. • Flagstaff, AZ 86001 • 928-233-3206 • www.Lowell.edu
and
**The Mount Washington Observatory** *(home of the worst weather recorded on Earth)*
PO Box 2310 • North Conway, NH 03860 • 800-706-0432 • shop.MountWashington.org

— William Lowell Putnam III
*Trustee emeritus*

*With especial gratitude to Dom Austen McNamee, OSB,*
*who gave early encouragement to this writer's deep curiosity.*

# Acknowledgments

In presenting this opus, this grateful scribe has enjoyed significant and often unwitting help from many others — both in association with the aforementioned observatories and from elsewhere. None of them deserve any blame for errors of fact, taste, or expression herein, though some of them managed to eliminate a few of the ones they found.

But in alphabetical order (though not necessarily by the value of their input), they are: Lauren Elizabeth Amundson, Lowell Observatory librarian; Marcia Bartusiak, professor of science history at MIT; Buddha Basnyat, president of the International Society of Mountain Medicine; Lawrence Peter (Yogi) Berra, baseball catcher and manager, *emeritus*; Edward Leonard George Bowell, Lowell astronomer *emeritus*; Morgan Andrew Broman, my computer literate stepson; Kirk Bryan (1888–1950), Harvard professor of geomorphology; Joseph Brooks Dodge (1898–1973), refounder of the Mount Washington Observatory; Otto Gustav Franz, Lowell astronomer *emeritus*; Johann Wolfgang (Hans) Gmoser (1932–2006), skier and mountain guide; Samuel Harlow Goodhue (1920–2006), engineer and philanthropist; Jeffrey Clifton Hall, Lowell Observatory Director; David Chalmers Henley, geophysicist of Calgary; Scott Henley, executive director of the Mount Washington Observatory; Padraig John Houlahan, one-time Lowell Observatory IT manager; David Peter Jones, explorer, scientist, and writer; Andrew John Kauffman II (1920–2002), diplomat and alpinist; Almyra Laberge, secretary of the Lowell Institute; George Wesley Lockwood, Lowell astronomer *emeritus*; Dom Austen McNamee (1908–1980), OSB, monastic teacher; Dee Molenaar, mountaineer, geologist, and artist; Michael Kenneth Mortimer, world traveler and retired alpinist; Robert Leslie Nichols (1904–1995), Tufts University professor of geology; Michael C. J. Putnam, professor *emeritus* of classics at Brown University; W. Lowell Putnam IV, this scribe's generally patient son; J. Kent Robinson, Lowell advisor and our backup photographer; the eminent journalist, David Starr, a respected competitor and old friend; Lawrence Harvey Wasserman, Lowell Observatory senior astronomer; and at the end — Dr. and Mrs. Thomas Callander Price Zimmermann: he, professor *emeritus* of Italian renaissance history and she, the daughter of a distinguished alpinist, this scribe's most respected associate, the late Dr. Benjamin Greeley Ferris Jr.

It would be most difficult to prioritize this list of helpers, but this scribe is especially grateful for the input from Dr. Franz, whose continental and classical background has given his comments, and corrections, much extra credibility and value. However, we have a particular fondness in our debt to this compiler's great, great-grandfather, the Reverend George Putnam (1807–1878), an eloquent preacher, a member of the Massachusetts Constitutional Convention of 1853, multi-year pastor of the First Church of Roxbury, Massachusetts, and a trustee of Harvard University. It is this ancestor's 1825 concordance of the King James Bible, the product of Alexander Cruden (1697–1770), which — handed down through four intermediate generations — has long enabled this compiler to readily cite Holy Scripture to substantiate an enormous variety of potentially conflicting viewpoints.

# Introduction

> *I have seen all the works that are done under the sun; and behold, all is vanity and vexation of spirit.*
>
> *That which is crooked cannot be made straight; and that which is wanting cannot be numbered.*[1]
>
> — Ecclesiastes, I:14–15 (KJB)

For close to half a millennium, a great many good Christian people have been brought up to place unchallengeable faith in the work and words of a group of Church of England theologians assembled by the order of King James I, who were collectively charged with researching all manner of ancient texts and other related data, and then to come up with a documented version of Holy Scripture on which all Christians (particularly the ones they cared about) could rely with confidence. This task began at the Hampton Court Conference in 1604, chaired initially by the aging Archbishop of Canterbury, John Whitgift (1530–1604), who had recently crowned James VI (Stuart) of Scotland as King of England, successor in 1603 to the long-lived younger daughter of Henry VIII, England's "Virgin Queen" Elizabeth (Tudor), who had reigned since 1558.

Hampton Court was a royal residence just outside London, constructed by the well-connected English prelate, Thomas Wolsey (1475–1530), alleged ultimately to have been a faithless agent of King Henry VIII, who then confiscated the premises. The membership of this ecclesiastic task force included a score of prominent and scholarly leaders of the Church of England, supplemented by a handful of the religious — and soon-to-be political — insurgents, known as Puritans (or Roundheads). There was, however, not a papist, a Presbyterian, nor a Celtic Irishman in the lot — though James, heritor of the papal designation "Defender of the [Christian] Faith," claimed to be the God-given ruler of them all. For better or for worse, the group's collective perspective was correspondingly less broad.

Archbishops of Canterbury had been royal appointees ever since the break with the Church of Rome when Henry VIII unsuccessfully sought papal consent to divorce Catherine of Aragon, the Spanish-born wife he had "inherited" from his late older brother, Arthur. Whitgift's sole predecessor had been Edmund Grindal. His most immediate successors were Robert Bancroft, George Abbot, and then William Laud (the rigidity of whose religious policies and actions did much to stimulate the major migration of moderately well-to-do Puritans to New England in the 1640s and 1650s).[2]

This enormous ecclesiastical research task was determined necessary by the new king because ties to the parent Church of Rome were increasingly tenuous when relations were not actually hostile.[3] A number of versions of the Bible were in various degrees of circulation (thanks to Johannes Gutenberg) throughout England, as well as the rest of Christendom, and they all varied in credibility, mostly because of conflicting "improvements" or "clarifications" inserted by prior (often medieval) scribes in making copies of earlier documents by hand. Some versions were thus carried forward from more reliable sources than others, and considerable disagreement evolved between them all on various minutiae of Christian dogma and theology.

The Church of Rome had done much to clear up part of this incipient morass of theistic conflict at the Council of Nicaea in 325 CE, presided over by the Roman Emperor Constantine. Among other things, this council formally suppressed several accounts of the life of Christ purportedly written by various apostles and disciples and endorsed the accounts of the four presently known evangelists. But all that was more than 1,000 years in the past, and not even halfway back to the Babylonian roots of creationist mythology.

The Hampton Court Conference's work was completed and the first copies of the "approved" Bible were printed in 1611,[4] a remarkably short time considering the depth of research proposed at the start, thereafter forming the factual foundation for the genealogical study and report authored by James Ussher (1581–1656), Archbishop of Armagh,[5] and issued in 1650. This lengthy and detailed arithmetic exercise determined the completion of the world (occasionally known by others, in later years, as planet Earth) to have occurred in the late afternoon of October 23 in the year 4004 BCE.

Nothing in all the words that follow is meant to denigrate the extensive calculations of Bishop Ussher, for we rely on them — at least in part — though his great undertaking was merely the first, not the only, such chronology. (Other, less well-known, Biblical chronologies by subsequent learned Anglicans include those of William Hales [1747–1831], published in 1812; John Jackson [1686–1763], published in 1752; and the French Jesuit, Denys Petau [1583–1652], published in 1627.) The one point that all these chronologies have in common is agreement on the factuality of certain events — meteorological, biographical, and otherwise — in ancient Judaic oral history (which was transmitted around desert campfires over numerous generations). However, exactly when — and sometimes even how — these events occurred still appears open to considerable discussion.

As we go along, it may be worth noting that almost all "primitive" peoples worshiped the Sun; it was obviously the source of all light, heat, and ultimately food. Modern man, being more "advanced" in thinking, has almost unanimously bypassed the Sun to what is believed to be the Sun's Creator; maybe we shall all see about that. Holy Scripture also tells us that God created man in His image and likeness. However, it can also be quite logically argued the other way around: that man has created God and given Him (or perhaps Her) our image and likeness. Certainly, a great many present-day monotheists have this very same opinion regarding the numerous deities associated with Greek, Norse, Roman, and other "mythologies."

Many modern scholars — some religious but mostly otherwise — take issue with but one word in the King James ("approved") Bible, which is found redundantly in chapter I of Genesis: "day." The king's learned savants might just as well have used the words "period" or "episode" with equal, if not greater, credibility and without loss of theological meaning. But they didn't. In any case, they offered no scriptural documentation to support the commonly supposed "fact" that those critical six "days" of Creation[6] were of equal length, sequential, or contiguous.

Instead, the compilers of this "approved" Bible unwittingly sowed the seeds of a never-ending discord that is increasingly evident between those who accept the accelerating progress of scientific knowledge and numerous diehard King James[7] Biblical literalists. This side of science is most particularly represented in the documented findings of paleontologists and their ilk, resulting in the growing public awareness, on the one hand, of astronomical, geological, climatological, and other scientific facts and processes.

This opus represents, in the seven chapters that follow, one scribe's attempt to bridge that wholly unnecessary intellectual gap; for all but the deliberately blind know, whether they admit it or not, that though the Bible says the world was "completed" more than 6,000 years ago, the face of the Earth is constantly undergoing re-Creation by various means — some subtle, some explosive, some meteorological, some human-caused, and some external.

• • •

This entire literary endeavor to separate Biblical literalism from observable reality was prompted by the fact that one supposedly erudite scholar managed to propound on American National Public Radio (with a presumably straight face) the "fact" that the Colorado River's Grand Canyon, a notable feature of the high plateau of Northern Arizona, was formed in one brief but eventful period of runoff when all the waters accumulated on Earth by the Great Flood associated with the Biblical patriarch, Noah, drained back into the ocean through this one channel — thus carving the canyon. At least, this "scholar" paid some obeisance to the process of erosion, though he may well be subject to review in his concepts of timing or geography. For anyone who cares to take the time and look closely can determine — given the observable rate of down-cutting and the total volume of material removed — that the ongoing carving of the canyon must have begun some thousands of millennia before the alleged globally catastrophic flood.[8] Moreover, if, as we are told, Noah's flood did cover "the whole face of Earth"— even, therefore, the highest of mountains — it would mean a worldwide oceanic depth of another five or more miles and thus require an off-planet storage facility for all that water when it was not needed for drowning the evil folk that God might happen to become displeased with.

Certainly, those residents of the eastern end of the Mediterranean Sea who finally wrote down the oral history legends that make up what most Christians call the Old Testament did not even know about the Grand Canyon — one-third of the globe away — or its newly supposed function in aid of Holy Scripture. They never had a chance to hear about the canyon's existence until sometime after 1561 AD, when Francisco Coronado and others first reported their discovery to folks in the Old World. Coronado reported to people in Spain, then in a state of major disagreement with King James, his predecessors, and their countrymen. Thus, word on this method of its origin and even the very existence of the Grand Canyon would have had much difficulty reaching any of the English scholars assembled at Hampton Court.

Complicating a literal acceptance of this part of Holy Scripture is the fact that apparently Noah, from whom all mankind is said to be descended, drifted about on the worldwide flood waters of 2348 BCE for two months in his divinely inspired ark. What all the passengers' lived on during this voyage is not specified (though the people at Carnival Cruises might learn a thing or two from insightful Biblical study), and the passengers seem to have all been in good health and spirits when they disembarked. There is no data on how such diverse creatures and fellow travelers with Noah as the arctic walrus and muskox, the Australian kangaroo and wombat, the Adelie penguin, the American bison, the tropical python (and perhaps even the Yeti or Sasquatch) managed to then get safely to their proper habitats[9] from the arid highlands of Eastern Turkey. As well, there is no explanation as to how Noah managed to avoid many mountains considerably higher than the nearly 5,000 volcanic meters of Mount Ararat, and those not too far away from it, before running aground.

A further complicating factor in this discussion is that the human spirit has great difficulty comprehending the finality of death. Death is a "fact of life" to which humans readily consign all of God's other creatures — not merely domestic creatures, but everything that we are led to believe was in the ark, as well as a good many foes[10] of Christianity. The list would have had to include everything from worms on up, including fleas, germs, mosquitoes, hundreds of different types of snakes, moose, broncos, brontosauruses, lions, antlions, hens, hyenas, and then some. But we cannot accept death for ourselves. For this widely held belief, abounding in the folklore of even the most pagan and "primitive" of human societies, has been the basis of every known society on the idea that there is an afterlife for us alone, the details of which take various forms depending on one's religious preferences. Worship of the Sun is therefore quite understandable, for — as almost every human society determined early on — our parent star really is the source of all heat, life, and weather on Earth.

A most often male and sometimes celibate priestly class, however, entry into which is granted only after a suitable period of indoctrination, has also evolved in every human society, whose members have assumed unto themselves, with near unanimous societal acceptance, the ability to speak authoritatively for their society's almighty but indefinite and indefinable source.

• • •

Considering the supposed education of an immense number of people, mostly in the United States of America, who deny the values and findings of science — at least insofar as they appear to disagree with the literal words of the King James or "approved" version of Christian Holy Scripture — it is remarkable that such folk feel able (without acknowledging any hypocrisy) to thrive, move about in, and try to assert considerable influence in today's science-based society. However, while they won't rush to discuss it, not one present-day Biblical literalist or preacher could even turn on the lights of his church without making use of the scientific findings of non-religious people such as Alessandro Volta, André-Marie Ampère, and Thomas Alva Edison. Not one televangelist or politician could preach his ignorance — or denial — of scientific fact without making use of the studies and applications of science variously attributed to Heinrich Rudolph Hertz, James Clerk Maxwell, Guglielmo Marconi, or even David Sarnoff and NASA. Hardly a clergyman (or politician) of any sort could get around in today's world without making use of the various implementations of science attributed to the initial work of Karl Friedrich Benz, the Duryea brothers, Rudolf Christian Diesel, the Wright brothers, or perhaps (if they have a greater taste for the comforts of Mammon) those originally made by Herr Benz for Ms. Mercédès Jellinek. Or if troubled with the physical ailments that afflict mankind, would any of those folk prefer to be repeatedly bled or deny themselves the benefits deriving from the painstaking studies attributed to Louis Pasteur, Maria Sklodowska (Marie Curie), Sir Joseph Lister, or Jonas Edward Salk?

In fact, precious few members of any modern or Christian society would not have trouble finding anything to eat without making use of the equally painstaking scientific improvements brought about in agriculture and animal husbandry by the studies of Friar Gregor Johann Mendel, Charles Darwin, and more recently by George Washington Carver and Luther Burbank. In the end, none of those folk named (or implied) — and we who follow — would ever be on time for anything without using the astronomical and geodetical conclusions spread among humanity by the scientific applications of Charles Dowd, Cleveland Abbe, and Sir Sandford Fleming.

The Scots-born Sir Sandford (1827–1915) was concerned about running a railway spanning the five present time zones of mainland Canada (almost a quarter of the circumference of Earth), and picked up the idea of horal conformity from the several British railways, all of which, from their very inception, ran every train on the time kept at the Royal Observatory in Greenwich. By way of contrast, prior to 1883, Charles Carroll's Baltimore & Ohio Railroad ran all the way to Chicago on Baltimore's astronomical time, and Commodore Vanderbilt's New York Central went to the same city (but to a different station) on the slightly different astronomical time kept at its Albany depot. Every railroad system was different, and good luck to those travelers who had to make connections between them.[11]

Most of the folk listed just above were also God-fearing (some of them very much so), at least for the record. However, in the end, even if we still have doubts — whether in this discussion as a devout believer, Biblical literalist, Creationist, educated skeptic, deist, atheist, or otherwise — everyone can always safely rely on the advice given by that well-known, contemporary philosopher of the practical,

Lawrence Peter "Yogi" Berra. He had a long and successful career chasing every flying foul ball near his home, as well as absorbing the pitches aimed in his direction from both left and right, and then uttered that timeless profundity: "You can observe an awful lot by just watching."

It is important, however, to be sure of the limitations of what you hope to be observing, as the famous Lone Ranger is reputed to have learned from his faithful Indian scout, Tonto:

> One evening, after an exhausting day spent chasing banditos in the New Mexico desert, the two men stopped and made camp. After they had prepared their campfire, eaten their small meal of beans and maize (or whatever cowboys and Indians ate during their frontier forays), tethered their horses Silver and Scout in the grass patch near the creek, and set up their tent, both men crawled inside and fell sound asleep. It had been a long day.
>
> Some hours later, Tonto nudged the Lone Ranger awake and gently asked him, "Kemo Sabe, look toward sky; what you see?"
>
> The Lone Ranger opened his eyes, inhaled a deep breath of the cool, desert air and responded: "I see thousands of stars."
>
> "What that tell you?" asked Tonto.
>
> The Lone Ranger, obviously a man of considerable intellectual attainment, pondered this query for a few long seconds and then slowly responded, "Astronomically speaking, it tells me there are hundreds of galaxies and potentially billions of planets. Astrologically, it tells me that Saturn is in Leo. Time-wise, it appears to be approximately a quarter past three in the morning. Theologically, the Lord is all-powerful, and all we humans are small and insignificant. Meteorologically, it seems we will have a beautiful day ahead of us. What's it tell you, Tonto?"
>
> The Indian scout raised himself up on one elbow, turned toward his companion, and said, "It mean you dumber than buffalo dung. Someone stole tent!"
>
> — Anonymous

• • •

It is also a fact that the most respected scientists, whatever their disciplines, readily admit that their knowledge is incomplete — particularly regarding their own specialties. On the other hand, almost all professional practitioners of religion have great difficulty in accepting any detail relative to their self-selected specialty that comes from a source other than one of their own choosing. Such folk already have all the answers they need and don't care to be bothered by extraneous data. The basic message of the opus that follows is that useful science and sensible religion can coexist quite gracefully, as long as neither party denies the right, privilege, or duty of the other to "do its thing" for the common benefit of all.

As stated at the outset, what follows is neither a work of philosophy nor of scientific argument. What follows is mostly a collection of pertinent facts. Please accept it as only that.

# I

# Recent Geological History

*He cutteth out rivers among the rocks; and his eye seeth every precious thing.*
— Job XXVIII: 10 (KJB)

The following tale is often told in beginner college geology classes. The great Swiss-born paleontologist Jean Louis Rodolphe Agassiz (1807–1873), closely associated with Harvard University for the last part of his notable career, was hiking through a rural suburb of Boston one afternoon with a group of his friends. One of them noticed a rocky outcrop that glistened strongly in the waning autumn sunlight and called it to the group's attention. Upon observing the rock — a roche moutonée[1] — Agassiz commented, "Where I was born [Canton Fribourg, Switzerland], if we saw such a rock, we would know there had been a glacier here."

Agassiz thus established in the New World what he had already done much to expound in the Old. His adult career had started with the study of medicine, but his interests drifted into the lore of ancient fishes, and he received much commendation for his paleontological work in Teutonic Europe. After visiting England in 1834 and turning the attention of savants there to the likely former presence of glaciers in Great Britain, he received a grant from King Wilhelm IV of Prussia[2] in 1846 that enabled him to travel to America late the following year. There he became the guest of John Amory Lowell (1798–1881), then sole trustee of Boston's unique Lowell Institute,[3] who had engaged him to deliver a series of twelve lectures on "The Plan of Creation — as Shown in the Animal Kingdom."[4]

Agassiz's royal benefactor (1795–1861), who had fled from Napoleon in his early youth, was a noted patron of science, but in 1861, he was judged insane and dethroned — as had been the fate of his older cousin in England, George III, some

*Right:* Louis Agassiz, the unintentional father of modern glacial geology, when he came to America. He remains one of the all-time great figures of scientific discovery. *From a poster at Brig, Switzerland, by W. L. Putnam III.*

*Below:* The Agassizhorn, at 3,946 meters in the massive limestone uplift of the Bernese Oberland, is 1 kilometer northwest of the more impressive Finsteraarhorn (4,274 meters). While some have shied away from extolling Agassiz in recent years, because of his allegedly racist views, the Swiss government remains proud of one of its greatest exports. *W. L. Putnam III.*

fifty years earlier. Fortunately, the great Swiss polymath stayed on in America — mostly in New England, though visiting elsewhere — and established a social, scientific, and educational legacy that came to include many of the most prominent American and European figures of knowledge, culture, and industry during the next century. That first Lowell Institute lecture (1840) opened with a declaration of humble scientific intent:

> The time has past when it was possible to doubt that there is order in Nature, when the existence of a general system regulating the whole Creation could be questioned. However, it has only been step by step that Man has acquired an insight into this plan. Knowledge was to be gained before this wonderful arrangement of Nature could be understood. And it was not at once fully understood. Understanding has been acquired gradually, successively and with difficulties. However, now we have sufficient data to be able to satisfy ourselves that the various views which have been brought forward respecting the order of Nature are not altogether fanciful, that they are not mere artificial means to assist us in our investigations. We can be satisfied that they correspond more or less to Nature. We have the positive hope that they will one day correspond to the natural phenomena, when we see how the investigations which are carried on in different directions by different authors go on, converging gradually, assisting each other, and harmonizing subjects which at first seemed entirely obscure, if not entirely inaccessible.

The final lecture, delivered in late January (1840), concludes with the following paragraph:

> The few hints which I have been able to give are only indications towards what is to be done. The comparison, step by step, between the various fossils of all Geologic periods — between the great changes which all families undergo, step by step — remains to be done, and then the plan of Creation will be better understood. Then we shall more fully acquire an insight into these harmonies, by which the whole is combined and carried through the ages to the perfection which has allowed Man to stand at the head of Creation.

Agassiz thus began the recognition, and subsequent scientific study, of glacial and related phenomena in the American Northeast. British and other European

The well-known Madison Boulder is a large feature that was glacially transported from one side of town to the other. It is the biggest thing going in the little-known township of Madison, New Hampshire. *Brian K. Fowler.*

geologists, however, with a bow to their religious contemporaries, had long been using the term "drift" to denote surficial deposits (including immense, megaton boulders) for the derivation and placement of which they could think of no other explanation than that they had been cast about in the enormous, watery turmoil felt to have been caused by the Biblical flood associated with the ark-building patriarch, Noah. Presumably, these numerous non-buoyant items were slithered into place during the time that Noah was drifting about in his ark prior to making a landfall on Mount Ararat. Thus the "scientific" literature of the eighteenth century often made use of the word "antediluvian" to indicate events or items that appeared to predate this legendary, worldwide inundation.

Apparently, by the time of Noah, God had become so disappointed with the behavior of all the terrestrial creatures He had created (though we could find no scriptural documentation of this universal damnation against the "lesser" creatures), that He was determined to pretty much start over. However, God seems to have had no issue at all with whatever lived in the water, so He did not call on Noah to do anything for them, and the fish probably did not suffer much from the resulting flood anyhow.

• • •

Though initially contested by the devout, by the mid-nineteenth century, the blossoming science of geology was given a strong, though unintentional, boost in credibility by the belated publication, in 1859, of Charles Darwin's *On the Origin of Species*. Darwin (1809–1882), a grandson of the famed pottery maker Josiah Wedgwood, rightly feared the controversy that would — and did — erupt. So he hesitated for some twenty years after his eye-opening, five-year-long voyage with Robert FitzRoy (a great grandson of King Charles II and a founder of scientific meteorology) on the *Beagle* before going public with the findings he had formulated on "natural selection." This scientifically oriented voyage (which lasted from 1832 to 1836) was promoted by the Royal Society, which was founded in 1660 by Christopher Wren soon after King Charles II returned from exile in Holland. The Society was later dominated by the great Sir Joseph Banks (1743–1820), who had toured the world with Captain James Cook from 1768–1771 in the *Endeavor*. Banks then became the Society's leading light, as well as a correspondent and friend of Benjamin Franklin (a very minor and simple fact that was of critical importance to British societal acceptance of the nascent American nation).

Meantime, across the English Channel — La Manche, to those on the south side — the French were also accepting modern notions under their "Sun King," Louis XIV, who was importing congenial savants from wherever he could get them (mostly Renaissance Italy) to enhance a domestic movement that became known as the French Enlightenment. Foremost among the native French philosophers was Denis Diderot (1713–1784), a sometime art critic and protégé of the Czarina Catherine II (the Great), whose vast personal library was "sold" to the German-born czarina and shipped to St. Petersburg after his death. Diderot coined many a resonant phrase, and although denied a place among the Sun King's intimate coterie, he is known, among other things, for having most clearly enunciated the process by which all valid scientific knowledge is gained:

> There are three principal means of acquiring knowledge available to us: Observation of nature, reflection, and experimentation. Observation collects facts; reflection combines them; experimentation verifies the result of that combination.[5]

The Enlightenment, which had its roots in the Italian Renaissance, came to enjoy ever greater public acceptance when a series of mostly British gentlemen-geologists, many of whom became incidental alpinists, began to apply present-day nomenclature to the localities where they found evidence of one-time living creatures in various ancient sediments (which were somehow lifted high above the ocean depths in which they had obviously been originally deposited). Being, for the most part gifted with classical educations, these men generally applied names taken from Latin or Greek to the various fossils and sedimentary rocks they studied. The most obvious descendant — in a reasonably direct line — of these early creatures is today's horseshoe crab, whose ancestry as a trilobite reaches back almost a billion years to the late Cambrian Era.

In order of seniority, these various rock formations and their times of derivation became formalized as Cambrian, after the Latin name for Wales, where a lot of early geologists worked; Ordovician, after the rocks best exposed in the North Welsh tribal turf of the Ordovices (when life first appeared on land); Silurian, for those exposed stratigraphically higher, in the south Welsh turf of the Roman Silures; and Devonian, for those somewhat younger rocks first studied in Devonshire. Rock formations with a high level of coal or other residual carbon were called Carboniferous. The name Permian was applied to rocks best exposed farther afield in the ancient Russian kingdom of Permia. Those that were best defined in the Jura Mountains of ancient Burgundy became known as Jurassic, whereas those with a generally high concentration of calcium or chalk were called Cretaceous. Below (older than) the Jurassic and Cretaceous is the Triassic, known for the first appearance of dinosaurs, and named by Friedrich Augustus von Alberti (1795–1878) because of the typical three layers of rock from this age found in many parts of northern continental Europe. At the end of the Cretaceous period, the Moon really failed us in sweeping up celestial brickbats, and a massive meteorite impacted Earth, apparently near the Yucatán peninsula. It kicked up a lot of debris into the atmosphere and abruptly terminated the Age of the Dinosaurs, most of whom were getting too big, anyhow, and were about to run out of food.

The early geologists (also known as natural historians) soon began to note that almost everywhere they looked, many of the older rocks in the surface layers of Earth had been bent, twisted, baked, lifted, broken, depressed, burnt, scraped, and variously abused by processes unknown and unreported in Holy Scripture. This is understandable, given that, with three brief and miraculous[6] exceptions, the ancient Hebrew fireside narrators appear to have had minimal contact with the oceans or volcanic action, and none at all with earthquakes — unless it was a fortuitous tsunami[7] that hit the Red Sea at the time of Moses's crossing, and a "quake," not the cacophony of various musical instruments, that caused the walls of "pagan" Jericho to crumble after Caleb's preliminary trip of espionage into the already occupied but more recently named Promised Land. After all, the geologists who have since studied the critical local aquifer tell us that the African plate has been shoving

Petra, a pre-Biblical temple carved into the reddish, Paleocene, Nubian sandstone of southern Jordan. *U.S. Geological Survey.*

into the European plate for quite a few millennia, and the wide-spread Nubian sandstone that underlies the entire Biblical region has been undergoing an uplift combined with periods of deposition throughout much of the past billion years.

In due course, by the process of locating the same kinds of fossil remnants in one part of the world as were found in another, prehistoric patterns began to emerge, and maps were prepared of the world at various stages of its history up to modern times. Though this whole historical research process had largely begun in Wales, the preferred modern locality for study of the development of Earth's most ancient forms of vertebrate life is among the long (time-wise) series of fossils found in the extensive Burgess shale formation of Western Alberta.

Some of Earth's older rocks (those nearest the bottom in any series of deposits) were found to be so mauled and deformed that they obviously belonged to a special category of antiquity that was initially called (mostly for momentary lack of a sufficient timeline) Pre-Cambrian, and they are best viewed in unique locations such as the innermost areas at the very bottom of the Grand Canyon. But younger, and generally less durable, rock formations also got relocated, time-wise, into formations broadly grouped later under the general category of Cenozoic, later combined in a period featuring more exalted continental elevations and occasionally cooler global temperatures known as the Pleistocene (classical Greek for "most recent"). For better or for worse, this is pretty much where we are now.

The early geologists also began to group (collectively) the several post-Archean eras into the Paleozoic (ancient life), Mesozoic (middle life), and Cenozoic (recent life) categories. Each was punctuated by developmental hiatuses between, now believed to have been caused by major meteorite impacts that made life impossible for those unfit to survive in the temporarily turgid atmosphere that resulted. Rocks were sometimes also called primary (crystalline or igneous in origin), secondary (sedimentary and/or metamorphic), and tertiary (less firmly consolidated and/or loose).

In any discussion of what came before man began keeping discernible records, it is useful to peruse a time table of Earth history, as has been deduced and recorded by scientists such as Monsignor Lemaître, Louis Agassiz, V. M. Slipher, and a horde of other astronomers and geologists.

Residents of North America do not need to comprehend the quite youthful geological origin of Niagara Falls, though it is a most interesting and complex story. They can see ample leftover evidence of the one-time continental glaciers of the Pleistocene in the form of the Grand Banks, the bouldery ridges and sandy inlets of Cape Cod, Nantucket, Martha's Vineyard, and Long Island; the extended lobate dams that hold back Lakes Erie and Michigan from their "normal" drainage southward to the Gulf of Mexico; and more importantly to current human society (although less topographically obvious), the fertile farmland of Iowa, Kansas, Saskatchewan, and adjacent areas. This deep loess soil is the result of the strong katabatic[8] winds and the consequent dust storms that blew over the bare ground that was freshly exposed when all that ice slowly melted away and all that water flowed back into the ocean, closing off the several land bridges from Asia and affecting much of the animal life later found in Australia and the Americas.

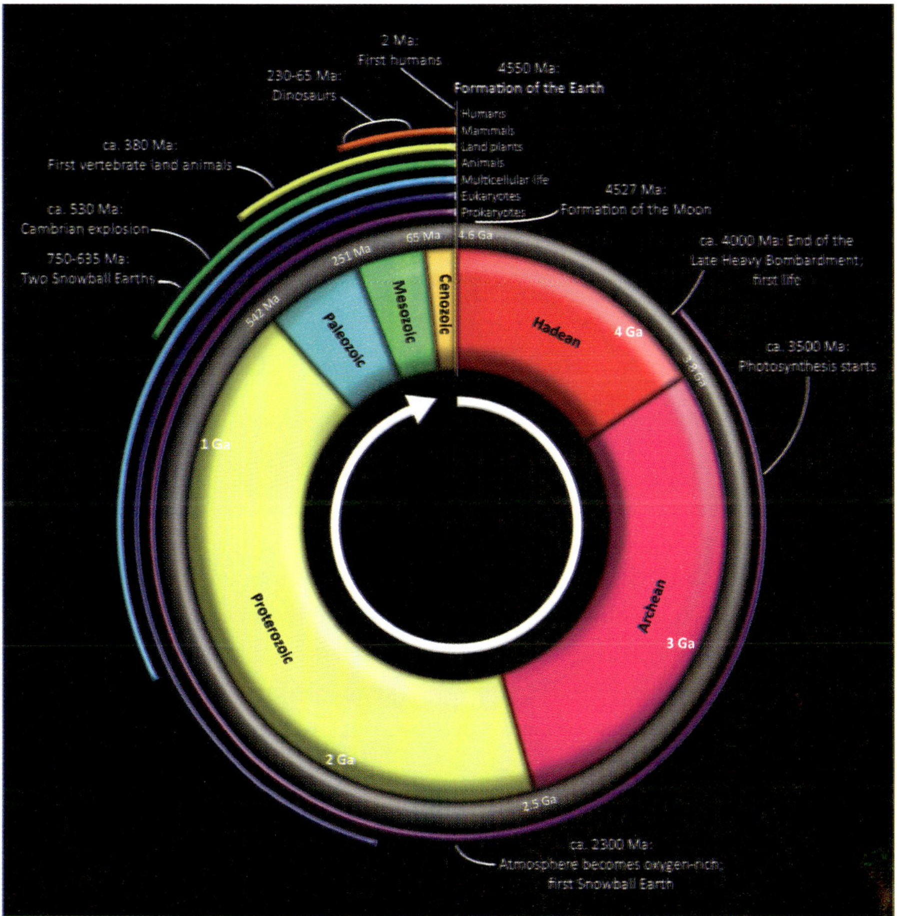


The times given in this geological clock are in approximate years "Ma" (a million years [Mega year] ago) and "Ga" (a billion years [Giga year] ago).

As the glaciers melted away, they left some landmarks, other than those named earlier. Massive glaciers often become overloaded with debris in the form of lenticular piles under the ice. These sturdy piles were up to 200 feet in height and streamlined to match the glacier's direction of flow; they are called drumlins. Wisconsinan glaciation in the northeastern United States left hundreds of them, but the most visible today are those in the area near Boston, where such landmarks as Bunker, Breeds, and Beacon Hills remain prominent, while some of those a bit farther east — out in the harbor — have not fared as well from the erosion accompanying the rise in sea level.

Local legend has it that a seventeenth-century ship captain named Nix was

A rocky shoal is all that presently remains of the island where Nix's mate was hanged. In 1636, it was reported to be a twelve-acre island, home to a flock of sheep. *U.S. Coast Guard.*

murdered at sea, and when his vessel returned to Boston, everyone accused his first mate of the act. Guilty or not, he was sentenced to be hanged on an island at the harbor's northeast entrance, and the body left "swinging in the wind" as a warning to other would-be malefactors. The mate died protesting his innocence and predicted the island would soon disappear as proof of his judges' error. The island shown on early charts has an area sufficient to support a large flock of sheep, but by the end of the eighteenth century, it was much reduced in size. By the end of the twentieth century, it was completely invisible at high tide, save for a masonry square bearing a beacon that was erected on what is now a bouldery shoal, most often seen latterly by those patronizing Logan Airport.

Comparable evidence of one-time glaciers is also available in Europe, where the mostly sandy peninsula of Jutland and the islands of modern Denmark represent a pile of moraine pushed ahead of a vast ice mass centered to the northeast in what we now call the Baltic Sea. The fertile soils of the lower Danube Valley and Ukraine were derived from katabatic winds blowing off the waning Würm Ice Sheet. That place name derives from its type locality in Bavaria, where this most recent stage of Pleistocene glaciation was first identified and studied. The corresponding deposits in North America from this fourth major episode of Pleistocene glaciation are called Wisconsinan, after its type locality.

This is by no means a complete recitation of the remnant landmarks pertinent to Pleistocene glaciation. Europe has many, and Helgoland, a small island off the northwest coast of Germany, has been sustained by heroic breakwaters and other measures used for decades in order to forestall a fate similar to that of Captain Nix's mate.

# God's Mechanisms

*He hath compassed the waters with bounds, until the day and night come to an end.*

*The pillars of heaven tremble and are astonished at his reproof.*

— Job XXVI:10–11 (KJB)

We do not plan to dissertate on the mechanisms by which planet Earth came into being — some things are beyond our mortal comprehension and belong more properly in the realm of study pertinent to the late Monsignor Georges Lemaître, president of the Pontifical Academy of Sciences. Furthermore, there are ample scholarly works on the subject. Cosmologists, headed a century ago by such luminaries as Sir James Hopwood Jeans (1877–1946), the American alpinist/geologist Thomas Chrowder Chamberlin (1843–1928), and their successors, pondered the geological and astronomical evidence available to man and then wrote extensively on their speculative concepts. But among the mechanisms, or agencies, that God seems to have used to alter the surface of planet Earth and adjust its habitability for various species of life from time to time are:

**1. Occasional meteoritic impact.** Since its possible gravitational capture as a closely passing asteroid some billions of years ago, Earth's Moon has done a passable job of sweeping up much of this kind of celestial debris from our near vicinity, as the uncounted "ding" marks on its surface indicate. (This is not the most popular current theory about the origin of Earth's Moon, but we happen to like it. And in the absence of definitive evidence to the contrary, it is as good as they get, for it also helps to explain Earth's rotational wobble [see chapter VII]. We do not, however, advocate the idea of green cheese as being the sole lunar content, of which [among other things] the late Neil Armstrong could find none.) Meantime, the center of the combined Earth/Moon mass, despite the 239,000± mile [400,000± kilometers] distance between them, is still within the main planet. This is unlike the situation of far-off Pluto, whose principal moon, Charon (with 12 percent of the total mass, and four more smaller moons), brings the center of the Pluto system to outside the parent, thus giving the main planet's rotation somewhat of a "dumbbell" effect. Furthermore, geological evidence observable on Earth itself indicates that large-scale and sometimes catastrophic meteor impacts seem to have occurred on our home planet in such places as central Ontario, off the Yucatán Peninsula, eastern and western Siberia, Australia, South Africa, and even near the Grand Canyon — not to mention those that must have created quite a splash when they landed in the ocean.

However, the Moon has also had an enormous positive impact on the development of life on Earth. Its gravitational effect on Earth's oceans has been largely credited by paleontologists with the slow evolution of organisms well suited to survive and thrive in the brackish muck of tidal estuaries before ultimately adapting further so as to prosper on dry land.

**2. Variations in solar energy output.** The Sun appears to be an unusually stable and noneventful star, but considering its current, eleven-year, "normal" cycle of sunspot eruptions, its energy output is still far from constant, as the record of post-Renaissance astronomers and various earlier and secondary diaries demonstrate. For lack of a suitable measuring system, astronomers are still quite unsure of the constancy of solar output in the more distant past.

**3. Glaciers.** Having melted away, glaciers leave behind a plethora of evidence of their one-time presence, which includes such things as extensive sand and gravel deltas, varved clays (the province of Dr. Antevs; see chapter VI) in one-time lake beds, tree-ring distortions and stump remnants (the province of Dr. Douglass), and pollen and leaf detritus, as well as the scars and scratches left by their grinding passage over the bedrock. Air molecules trapped deeply in residual ice bodies have yet another, but corroborative, story to tell about atomic half-lives and other such data as the amounts of carbon$_{14}$, beryllium$_{10}$, and carbon dioxide that were in Earth's atmosphere at the time of entrapment in the preserving medium of ice.

**4. Continental drift.** This hypothesis (made credible initially by the matching coastal outlines of western Africa and eastern South America and advanced originally by Alfred Wegener[1] early in the twentieth century, only to be widely scoffed at by his peers)[2] was revived and effectively demonstrated as actual by John Tuzo Wilson later in the century. Wilson found telling elements of past togetherness

in the bedrock geology of West Africa and eastern Brazil. Major, or even quite minor, shifts in land-mass alignment — such as the possible closing of the relatively shallow strait[3] separating Cuba from Florida or depressing the quite recently elevated (geologically speaking) Isthmus of Panama — might also have dramatically influenced the heat-distributing action of ocean currents.

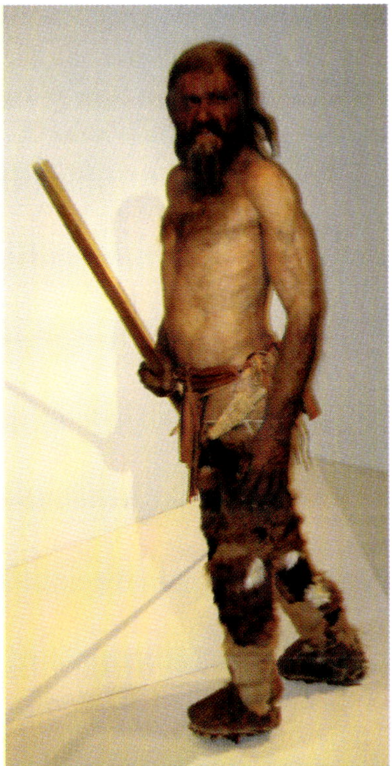

Glaciers were traversed by Ötsi, an itinerant of several thousand years ago, now frozen in a Bolzano museum. *W. L. Putnam III.*

**5. Various other erosive agents.** These include wind and moving water, which are indirect agents of solar-influenced diurnal weather and carry erosive subagents like sand and vegetative fragments. Water, in the form of snow and ice, is also an extremely powerful force in eroding or fracturing the bedrock and, as a glacier, in moving huge masses of rock and debris from place to place. The Sun itself, by imparting its daily heat to rock surfaces, causes selective expansion among the various crystal elements within any rock, from granite and gabbro to shale. In conjunction with recurrent nighttime cooling, it also causes the exposed layers to lose cohesion, crumble, and degenerate. This is why the surfaces, particularly of crystalline igneous rocks in sunlit desert areas, tend to become crumbly, rounded, and more easily abraded, whereas those exposed in areas more subject to greater rain and frost action tend to be firm, angular, and crisp.

**6. Tectonic displacements.** The internal heat of Earth increases with depth all the way down to its semi-molten core. If recurrent volcanic ejecta is not sufficient proof of this fact, this heat can also be deduced by noting the rise in temperature as one descends into deep mines or lengthy tunnels under mountain masses. The same fact has been deduced and expounded on by many seismologists[4] from the behavior of earthquake waves as they travel through the interior of the planet.

According to the adherents of Tuzo Wilson, the violent and spectacular aspects of volcanic activity we all know about are fundamentally the result of one of two factors. The first is the slow movement of continental plates over deeper-seated "hot spots" in the interior core of Earth (namely, the Central Pacific plate, containing the Hawaiian Islands, moving slowly to the west-northwest.[5] The second is the enormous heat generated by the collision of other plates with consequent subduction and orogeny — namely Mount St. Helens, Mount Fuji, and Mount Etna, the last of which (besides being a mainstay of crossword-puzzle makers) represents the output from the northward press of the large African plate and its collision with the European plate. This process is thereby — ever so slowly — squeezing out the Mediterranean Sea and pushing up the Alps and the other ranges of Europe that already show much evidence of being shoved upward and folded in the manner of a thick rug being pushed from one edge.

Another of these tectonic displacements, evidenced by the line of Pacific Coast volcanoes — Garibaldi, Rainier, Adams, Hood, Shasta, and so on — is a result of the westward motion of the North American plate, pushing into and under that of the North Pacific while simultaneously separating itself from Europe (at the rate of about one centimeter per century). Therefore, this process is also creating a volcanic rift in the mid-Atlantic, which is filled by magma rising from below that

Mount St. Helens was named for the British diplomat Alleyne Fitzherbert, Baron St. Helens (1753–1839). Here it is seen a few weeks after its top blew off in 1980. *Dee Molenaar.*

has accumulated enough to be represented by Iceland and the extended ridge of sea mounts and islands stretching southward to near the equator.

There is also evidence of crustal shortening, as well as crustal lengthening, within North America, which could have had climatic impact in past millennia. Between the uplift of present-day Colorado and the Cascade and Sierra Ranges of the Pacific Coast is a wide area where block faulting seems to have resulted from a stretching of Earth's surface. However, in Southern Alberta and Northern Montana, there is much evidence of the reverse effect to be found in the celebrated Lewis Overthrust Fault, which seems to have been caused by crustal compression, as the North American plate crunched into that of the North Pacific. This fault was recognized by geologist Bailey Willis (1857–1949) in 1902. Prior to his determination of this crustal shortening of up to 50 miles (80 kilometers), historical geologists were at a severe loss to understand how fossils that everywhere else were known to be of Cambrian Age in northwesternmost Montana were found resting conformably above formations that contained vastly younger fossils of the Cretaceous Age.[6]

Slightly farther north, this compressive process is what has caused the Canadian Rockies around tourist-prone areas such as Banff to manifest their deformation by faulting into a repetitive series of "writing desk" mountains where the thicker and more durable Eldon and Cathedral limestone formations of the Cambrian Age (as well as a couple of younger, Devonian formations) are repeated numerous times, standing firm as ridge lines with severe drop-offs to the east-northeast and also in more gentle southwestern approaches.

Many budding American geologists — particularly those who studied under Benjamin Silliman (1779–1864), his son and namesake at Yale, or the successors of Agassiz at Harvard — had trouble accepting the derivation of the highly deformed Paleozoic formations found throughout New England and the Maritime Provinces as being of sedimentary origin from the erosion of mountain masses "to the east." Obviously, all that lay to the east was the Atlantic Ocean, hardly an appropriate source. However, continental drift — very gradually shifting major surficial masses around on Earth's more plastic, almost-fluid inner layers and carried on for sufficient millennia — turns out to be a handy explanation for this otherwise insoluble dilemma. It is worth noting, while on the subject of plate tectonics, that this branch of geology is one of the most actively evolving areas of science, and many of the details that we presently rely on may be altered by subsequent findings.

• • •

God has used further, and generally lesser, mechanisms to tamper with Earth's climate from time to time. These include:

**1. Seemingly minor variations in energy output from the Sun.** These are more constant and frequent than we notice, have differing impact depending on their ionic content, and form some of the discussion of chapter VII.

**2. Intermittent volcanic activity**. This includes the explosion of Mount Mazama (Crater Lake)[7] in 5700± BCE, the explosive loss of the top 4,000 feet of Tambora in 1815 that caused New England to experience the "year with no summer" (coincidentally, this was the central year of the Dalton minimum of sunspot activity, a decidedly unfortunate combination for earthly agriculture), the explosion of Krakatoa in 1883,[8] the birth and eruption of Parícutin in 1943, and the revived activity of Mount St. Helens in 1980. They have all had their temporary effects on the global atmosphere and the regional or local climate, living organisms, and landforms — but none had long-term, global impact.

**3. Activities of organisms (not including man).** Principal among these is the strong likelihood that Earth's unique supply of oxygen (the basis of almost all presently known forms of life) was originally the product of enormous hordes of ocean-dwelling, amoeba-like creatures.

**4. Man.** This now ubiquitous latecomer to managerial status on planet Earth has had two forms of impact. The first occurred before the Industrial Age and prior to the widespread development of selective agriculture that has happened during the past two or three centuries. Man has "increased and multiplied" so as to become vastly more dominant and begun to crowd out all manner of "lesser species." The Reverend Thomas Robert Malthus (1766–1834) warned about this issue more than 200 years ago in his "Essay on the Principle of Population" and was ignored.

Meantime, bears of various types are but one egregious example of man's self-centered and unthinking impact on the rest of nature. Ursinae — whether Black, Brown, Grizzly, Kodiak, Panda, Polar, Sloth, or Sun — all require a much greater degree of privacy in which to live and reproduce than the ever-encroaching "needs" of mankind will allow. Humans continually move in on the bears' dwindling turf — whether for highway building, adventure tours, mineral or oil extraction, or summer homes — and then claim that the nearsighted bears are marauders and should be exterminated. It ain't fair to the rest of God's creatures; the process is shortsightedly selfish and encourages man down its own primrose path to extinction. Unless we get suddenly smarter, or something intervenes, before very long, we will have occupied, for one humanly desirable purpose or another, every bit of productive space on this planet. Our successors will

assuredly then have to face Armageddon-style lebensraum issues, commodity shortages on a global scale, and a societal collapse of worldwide extent. Just look at the facts! Planet Earth simply cannot sustain the present rate of human increase and resource usage.

Second, with man's gradual development of agriculture, some 10,000 or so years in the past, many previously forested areas were increasingly converted to grasslands (or deserts), which offer a much different actinic-ray reflectivity and water-retention capability than did the earlier forests.[9] Before this development, man had minimal environmental impact, since our earliest ancestors appear to have been hunter-gatherers, living in African trees or caves, eating the available fruits and nuts. They had not yet stumbled into the Garden of Eden, where they began to seriously "increase and multiply" following that famous Biblical mandate, which is manifestly impossible for all of God's creatures to fulfill or sustain.

Since man began the widespread burning of fossil fuels — some 250 years ago, first with coal, then oil and natural gas[10] — to do his work, keep warm in the winter, or cool in the summer, the impact on Earth's gaseous atmosphere has been substantial. Indeed, it is hard to imagine anything fundamentally sillier than building a big fire in order to keep cool. But when you get right down to it, air conditioners run on electricity, and most of the world's electricity is generated by coal-fired steam turbines; numberless tons of coal are burned every day. Thus, not to become diverted into discussion of the equally threatening rise of the methane level, the carbon dioxide content of Earth's air is now more than 40 percent greater than it was two centuries ago and rising at an accelerating rate. We know this from careful laboratory examination of cores drilled deep into mountaintop glaciers in the Andes as well as in Antarctica and Greenland. There is no evidence in analysis of the air trapped in such ice bodies that, despite ongoing volcanic ejecta, Earth's atmosphere has ever had the current level of carbon dioxide concentration at any prior time in the past million years.

The question thus arises about the tipping point at which this atmospheric pollution develops into the runaway condition that is apparently operative on our perpetually cloud-covered sister planet, Venus, where the carbon dioxide content of the gaseous atmosphere is so high — and thus so retentive of heat — that the temperature at its solid surface is hot enough to melt lead. This condition was discovered by the radio-telescope people at Arecibo, in Puerto Rico, who peered through the clouds and mapped the solid surface of our neighboring planet in 1958. Besides being Earth's closest celestial neighbor, size-wise Venus is nearly Earth's equal, except for its dense atmospheric mantle, mostly of carbon dioxide.

(While this scribe cannot escape some degree of inherited collateral responsibility for the public fascination with and the American space program's apparent concentration on Mars, mankind would do far better to devote more attention to what happens on Venus than to past events or possible living conditions on Mars.) Coincidentally, while this chapter was in early draft preparation, the *New York Times* (on December 24, 2012, page 4) reported extensively that "Antarctic Warming Is Speeding Up."[11] Nearly a year later, as this manuscript was receiving its final critical review by Professor Zimmermann, the *International Herald Tribune* offered a front page story on September 29, 2013, under the headline "UN Panel Sets Deadline for Action on Climate."

• • •

It is worth observing (per Mr. Berra's dictum) in this regard that, for all our supposedly advanced ingenuity, modern man is incapable of accomplishing anything necessary for maintenance of our supposedly sophisticated civilization — extending even to travel out of this world — without first creating a fire of some sort. When you think about it, this is not really much of an advance over what our ancestors did many centuries ago. However, due to our collective greed, lack of self-control, intense reliance on ancient hearsay, and general shortsightedness, maybe we deserve to become extinct.

A more homey proof of man's unintentional impact can also be inferred from somewhat younger Holy Scripture — in the Acts of the Apostles and the Epistles of St. Paul. Note that in approximately 555 BCE, the ancient Greek temple of Artemis at Magnesia, on the hillside north of the Meander River in Ionia, was destroyed by an earthquake (the African plate's slow northward movement in action). It was then rebuilt, of necessity with the use of smaller roof beams, as the bigger, older, trees on the hillsides above the Meander had all been harvested for this and other purposes. The ruins of the rebuilt temple (the victim of another earthquake) show that a set of interior pillars had to be erected to accommodate the shorter roof timbers then available.[12]

However, Acts XX: 16–17 also make it clear that St. Paul took ship from Miletus, then a port at the mouth of the Meander River, on his way, maybe with his usual sidekick, Barnabas, to visit with the Christian community at Ephesus (now Izmir) before ultimately finding his way north and west around the Aegean Sea to Corinth.[13] The port from which St. Paul sailed is now a good distance inland from the Aegean Sea, as the valley of the Meander (the actions of which also gave this river's name to a geomorphic fluvial process) has become ever more heavily silted by the runoff erosion caused by repeated cutting of the nearby timber to

Evidence of geological processes from Holy Scripture:
The port city of Miletus in 1994 (a), almost two millennia after St. Paul's visit. The lower valley of the River Meander has been filled with silt eroded from the now barren Ionian hillsides (c) to the north, which are dotted with Temple ruins (b). *W. L. Putnam III.*

burn, put roofs over various temples, and so forth. Herds of goats now graze on these increasingly barren limestone hillsides, thus — in the nature of most goats — keeping the vegetation ever more puny, and enhancing the process of silting up the riverbed, thereby forcing the river to snake around even further in its quest to reach the sea while also rendering Miletus no longer a seaport. (This scribe has waded across the muddy bottom of the barely hip-deep Meander, downstream from Miletus.)

Those who do not wish to rely on Christian Holy Scripture for this sort of unwritten historical fact can refer to the works of the Greco-Roman historian Polybius.[14] His account of the Second Punic War tells of the army of Publius Cornelius Scipio, which was unsuccessful in closing with Hannibal as he crossed the Rhône, north of Massilia, and then took a ship back to the port of Pisa, which is at the mouth of the Arno. Hannibal thereupon crossed the Alps with his twenty-eight elephants into Italy. Meanwhile, Scipio sent much of his army by sea to attack Hannibal's base in Spain. By the next summer (218 BCE), he had refitted his forces, which still outnumbered the Carthaginians, and though he eliminated the armored African elephants as a fighting force, he was killed himself before the Romans proceeded to lose every one of a fifteen-year series of battles fought across the length and breadth of Italy. The point of this digression is not to rehash the Second Punic War or Hannibal's route over the Alps, though the latter has been a favorite topic of speculative historians for centuries, but that Pisa was obviously once a significant port. Thanks, however, to human impact on the lands of the Arno basin, Pisa is now several miles inland, as unwise farming methods have caused the river to silt up its delta[15] so much that Livorno is now the local seaport.

A larger-scale example of this same process is found in the lower delta of the Mississippi River, where the port of New Orleans remains open to oceangoing vessels only through the sustained efforts of the United States Army Corps of Engineers. They finally adopted the advice of James Buchanan Eads (1820–1887), America's foremost civil engineer, and placed a series of jetties in Plaquemines Parish that force the "father of waters" to dump the silt it derives from the farms of America's Midwest so as to cause the river's current to keep the ship channel open for business.[16]

Even the most devout Bible thumper can believe these processes operate because, in a very small degree, St. Paul's biblically reported journeys prove the results of some, and though Holy Scripture is redundant or conflicting on many other matters, it is totally silent on geological processes. But mostly we know because, if we heed the advice of Mr. Berra, we can see some of these things happening before our very eyes, and thereby (because we saw something different going on at some precise spot last week, last year, when we were children, or often just by looking around after attentive reading of Holy Scripture or Roman history[17]) deduce what already took place, or was likely to happen, soon after.

• • •

Msgr. Georges Lemaître, a Belgian hero of the Great War who was also a physicist, astronomer, and papal advisor, was a famed cosmological theorist, shown here as a contemporary of Albert Einstein. *Lowell Observatory Archives.*

The process of erosion and consequent alteration of Earth's surface is continuous everywhere and was initially documented in glaciers by alpinists of many nations. It has been recorded with increasing consistency in the past three centuries, following the fuller impact of man's increasing use of carbon-based fossil fuels, beginning with the evolution of Thomas Newcomen's first steam engine in 1712.

However, it is difficult to leave the enormously (infinitely?) large topic of the formation of the Moon, Earth, the Sun, the Milky Way, the Andromeda Galaxy, and the vastness of the universe beyond without making a reference to the 1978 publication of Dr. Robert Jastrow,[18] who went on from his chapter on "Slipher, de Sitter, and Einstein" to suggest that since the expansion of the universe appeared (to him, anyway) to be slowing down, we may all be in for a gravitational contraction back to Monsignor Lemaître's original "primal atom." We just don't know when, but "soon" is clearly an unlikely answer, and besides, most cosmologists doubt very much that the expansion is, indeed, slowing.

Few among us are so brave or so farsighted as to theorize beyond the Belgian clergyman and papal advisor Georges-Henri Lemaître (1894–1966), an engineer and Allied hero of the Great War who became a diocesan priest at Louvain in 1923 at age twenty-nine, a few years before MIT awarded him a PhD. Lemaître then slowly formulated what he called the primal atom hypothesis, more commonly referred to by less sophisticated others as the big bang theory. An occasional

Italian machine-gun emplacement atop the Colle di Tenda. This was one of many military installations remaining in the Maritime Alps, designed to repel a French invasion from Savoy, which never came, thanks largely to effective British diplomacy.

colleague (or competitor) of Albert Einstein, Monsignor Lemaître earned the respect of everyone he met — from Pope Pius XI, Achille Damiano Ratti (1857–1939), and even his successor, Eugenio Pacelli (1876–1958), on down — by also expounding on the "simple" thought that there really isn't much practical difference between eternity and infinity.

Perhaps one reason why this scientist and this Pope got along so well, despite the traditional apprehension between some of their respective predecessors,[19] was that Ratti, besides being a learned librarian, was also a notable alpinist, who in his position as Pope, politely spurned the offer of honorary membership in The Alpine Club (though in response, he did say that he would have welcomed election as a regular member[20]). In his recreational mountaineering activities prior to election to the Papacy, Monsignor (later Cardinal) Ratti had frequent occasion to observe the strongest mechanism by which God has sculpted the face of Earth. He was thereby more inclined to understand these land-altering processes than most of his predecessors and, unfortunately, a good many of his contemporaries, as well as more than a few of his successors in religious leadership. Ratti and his clerical climbing team occasionally encountered units of the Italian Alpini on mountain training maneuvers — mostly in preparation for a potential French attack in the

Vesto Melvin Slipher was directed by his employer, Percival Lowell, to use a newly acquired spectroscope to determine the composition of the Andromeda Nebula — then suspected to be a solar system in formation. This patient and innovative observer subsequently determined that the color shift of Andromeda's spectrum indicated this dim collection of stars was moving at such a speed that the entire study of astronomy was thus very much revolutionized. *Lowell Observatory Archives.*

pre-1915 years when Italy was a sworn ally of Germany and Austria. The priests would administer the sacrament to the soldiers and then go climbing.

It is even more difficult for this scribe to leave this same topic, for Monsignor Lemaître's theoretical work was based very largely on the astronomical and extragalactic studies conducted on Mars Hill in Flagstaff by Dr. Vesto Melvin Slipher (1875–1969)[21] before he became the director of the Lowell Observatory, during which latter time he was visited in Flagstaff by the famed cleric to help see in the New Year of 1933.

Slipher has been very much overlooked until recent years, but many current astronomers feel that if Slipher had had the telescopic instrumentation available to Edwin Hubble — he used only a 24" refractor versus Mount Wilson's 100" reflector (Lowell's significantly larger 42" reflector was reserved exclusively for observations of the planets) — there is no limit to what he might have determined. As it was, within the astronomical community, he is commonly far more revered than his employer or any of his contemporary researchers in extragalactic matters. After Percival Lowell's death in 1916, everyone who was anyone in contemporary astronomy came to Flagstaff, Arizona, to converse with, and pump, the somewhat reticent Dr. Slipher — from Monsignor Lemaître through Henry Norris Russell, William Wallace Campbell, Jan Oort, and Gerard Kuiper to Edwin Hubble. The Santa Fe Railroad people must have been impressed, for its managers frequently stopped their "limited" express trains in Flagstaff for Percival Lowell and his distinguished visitors.

Climate change within "historic times" may also have escaped the attention of the famous English politician and historian Edward Gibbon (1737–1794), whose notable opus *The History of the Decline and Fall of the Roman Empire,* recounts authoritatively the series of invasions from migrant hordes coming from the east that toppled the empire of the Caesars and spread political and social chaos around Europe. However, Gibbon was unable to go back to his sources in sufficient depth to determine what it might have been that set these various invaders in motion.

That task remained for the Swedish explorer, Sven Anders Hedin (1865–1952), sent in 1885 by the King of Sweden to visit the Shah of Persia, after which he stayed on to travel around the vicinity of Samarkand in the presently arid region of central Asia. During this lengthy visit and subsequent trips, Hedin was able to determine there had once been a flourishing civilization (that even included libraries) in what was, at the time of his explorations near the close of the nineteenth century, a vast and chilly desert. With the help of some ancient Chinese records found in Tibet, Hedin determined that it was a serious change of the local climate that set in motion the exodus of many locals, some of whom became part

of the series of rapacious tribesmen, variously labeled in Europe as Tatars, Huns, Goths, Ostrogoths, Visigoths, Vandals, Franks, and finally Lombards, who rampaged their way toward the setting Sun following the lure of the fabled opulence of the setting empire.

At approximately the same time, other human records disclose that destructive Mughal hordes burst southward out of the Karakoram to overwhelm the more peace-loving prior natives of the Indian subcontinent. Barbarous Mongols stormed eastward from Mongolia and Tibet to barge in on and dominate the ancient civilization of China.[22]

It is only somewhat parenthetical to this subject to note that Samarkand was one of the locales wherein resided the great Persian poet/mathematician/astronomer Omar Khayyám (1048–1131), the poetic aspect of whose life was made famous by the British writer Edward Fitzgerald (1809–1883).[23] Khayyám, whose parental trade was tent making, described complex mathematical formulae, disputed Euclid, and helped devise the Iranian calendar, in which the earthly year — at a total of 365.24219858156 days — is far more precisely stated than it was by the scientists employed by either Julius Caesar or Pope Gregory XIII.

Hedin was one of four noted players in the Great Game of exploring Tibet and central Asia in the nineteenth century, somewhat on behalf of their respective governments. Lieutenant Colonel Sir Francis Edward Younghusband[24] did so, forcing the Dalai Lama to submit to a degree of British control. Sir Marc Aurel Stein[25] organized and led a series of "burglaries" into the lamaseries of Tibet, bringing home numerous artifacts for the British Museum in London. Somewhat contemporary was the Tsar's agent, Nikolay Miklovitch Przhevalsky (1839–1888), who planted the Russian flag most firmly in the region to the north of Tibet.

In his account of a trip across the Gobi Desert during the winter of 1927–1928, Hedin wrote about the lake Lop-Nor, from which one can see the holiest of Buddhist mountains, Mount Kailash Parbat,[26] the home of Shiva (of which the 52 kilometer circuit is nearly as much of a duty to believers as the Hadj is to devout Muslims) in the Gobi Desert. Lop Nor was fed by streams flowing northeast from the same Karakoram Range that had recently been visited by the Workmans, as mentioned below.[27]

> The southern lake, Kara-koshun, whose mean depth … amounted to 0.81 meters, fills with mud which the Tarim [river] carries with it, with decaying animal and vegetable matter, and with shifting sands, while the dried-up northern parts of the desert are hollowed out by the mighty force of the strong east-north-east storms and sink in the course of the centuries …

> I was thinking of this remarkable lake, which soon would become the most famous of all the lakes of the earth. That its wanderings were periodic I had proved, and the single period extended probably over one and a half thousand years … and this endlessly long trade route [Silk Road] led along the shore of Lop-nor. From this blessed lake or from rivers-tributaries [sic] and little lakes that are closely connected with their hydrographic system, merchants, their servants and animals, marching troops, and the members of embassies, could quench their thirst.
>
> At the beginning of the fourth century [Christian Era] Lou-lan perished, after it had been attacked and plundered by the barbarians living in the north. The threatening wars are spoken of by several of the documents that I found in the deserted town in 1901, and which have been translated and published by Professor Conrady[28] in Leipzig. But in other places, too, fortifications and villages completely disappeared, when, at approximately the same time, or a little later, the lake of Lop-nor dried up and wandered to the southern edge of the desert, after the Tarim, the Ho of the Chinese, had changed its course and dug out for itself a new bed towards the southeast and south. Men and animals fled towards the west and south, where the water flowed along; millions of fish and molluscs perished, and their dry bones and shells break now under our steps in the old watercourses, like fallen leaves in autumn. Death and oblivion lay like a shroud over the remains of the high culture of Lou-lan. When, not far to the south of this region, Marco Polo traveled along on his famous journey to the court of Kublai Khan, Lou-lan had been slumbering in its desert for nearly a thousand years, and the great Venetian had no idea of the former existence of this town …

Hedin went on to theorize about previous courses of this river, which becomes the Hwang Ho as it flows east from Tibet into the Sinkiang Province. He did not, however, indulge in an exercise in analysis of plate tectonics, which might have explained these events. Hedin was a generation ahead of Wegener (two generations ahead of Tuzo Wilson) and even more unaware of the fact that, a whole century later in 1999, Dr. H. Bradford Washburn (1910–2007), in one of his final exercises in precision surveying, determined that Mount Everest, at 29,035 feet above sea level, is still rising while moving northeastward quite rapidly (6± centimeters per year), as the tectonic plate of India crunches northward into the

The valley of the Indus River, in modern Pakistan, is cut into poorly consolidated sediments, shown here below the town of Gilgit and the high peaks of the Karakoram. *W. L. Putnam III.*

center of Asia, continuing to elevate the relatively youthful and less well consolidated rocks of the Himalayas and associated ranges.

Rivers are seldom permanent in one set course. This practice is particularly noted in their lower reaches, and when they change, it is invariably described by historians as a human catastrophe. Thus, we cite a more recent, although not current, authority — *Webster's Geographical Dictionary* (1963 edition) that says of the Huang He, or Yellow River:

> ab. 2700 m. long, N cen and E China, 2nd largest in country; navigable as far as Lanchow; rises in Amne Machin Shan, SE Tsinghai, at ab. 14,000 ft.; flows E and NE across Kansu, then N as E boundary of Ningsia; at 40°N makes a great bend flowing E across Suiyuan, Inner Mongolia, then S bet. Shensi and Shansi, receiving the Fen tributary from the E; at Tungkwan in E Shensi receives the Wei and turns directly E through gorges along N Hunan border. Its lower course across the Great Plains has shifted

> many times through the centuries, vitally affecting 35,000,000 acres of rich farmland; for more than 500 years before 1852 its outlet was the Yellow Sea in Kiangsu; from 1852 to 1938 its course was NE from near Kaifeng across Shantung past Tsinan to Gulf of Po Hai; again diverted, this time by Chinese military action against the Japanese invaders.

Contemporary sources, such as Wikipedia, are more fulsome in recitations of the human disasters inflicted by this historic river over the millennia of Chinese history. If one can disassociate one's thinking from the bathos, one can begin to accept that collectively, humanity is not all that important in the totality of Earth's history. In any case, the Yellow River is credited with bringing vast amounts of the loess mentioned by Hedin downstream to the flood plains of China. In so doing, this river (as well as its South China counterpart, the Yangtse) has routinely demonstrated that the carrying power of a river is directly related to the water's speed and volume, in consequence of which, after a spate, a river tends to drop its burden in its own bed, as well as dump the heaviest silt nearest its course when no longer in vigorous flood.

As a result, Chinese water engineers learned a flood control adage: "Dig the bed deep, and keep the banks low." Unfortunately, it is difficult to have a river both ways. The river's widespread flooding is a serious inconvenience, but the murky water of the flood does bring a replenishment of the soil, on the products of which everyone lives. So floods are good — as well as bad. And they occur with some regularity too.

After visiting the Mangnang Monastery,[29] in far southwestern Tibet, Hedin described another aspect of climate change:[30]

> And in the Sutlej[31] valley, the water has again acquired its rights. A new change of climate occurred, this time from drought to abundant precipitation. The transition must have extended through thousands of years. The precipitation increased slowly and steadily, perhaps with periodic interruptions. At last the southwest monsoon flooded the Himalayas with extraordinarily heavy deluges of rain. The water collected into mighty rivers that cut their channels vertically through the loess deposits of the steppe period. The result is wild, dissected canyon country on all sides.

III

# Before the Alpinists

*Only a few industrious Scots perhaps, who indeed are dispersed over the face of the whole Earth.*

— G. Chapman, *Eastward Hoe*, Act III, Sc. 2 (1605)

Most people will live their whole lives without ever encountering a glacier. Therefore, since this scribe has spent many days and weeks in close proximity to them, a few words of explanation are in order. In mountainous or arctic terrain, glaciers represent the slow accumulation of residual snow, unmelted by summer's heat and therefore accumulating in depth from year to year. Because ice behaves as a plastic under pressure, glaciers tend to slump downward and thus slowly move from regions of accumulation to lower, and generally warmer, valleys where they wither away from starvation and heat.

Without doubt, the foremost of the world's early authorities on glaciers (and much of geology in general) was a Scotsman, James David Forbes (1818–1868), whose volume *Travels Through the Alps of Savoy, and Other Parts of the Pennine Chain with Observations on the Phenomena of Glaciers* was first published in Edinburgh in June of 1843. The frontispiece of this notable work is a colored depiction of a glacier table on the Mer de Glace that illustrates, with dramatic impact, one of the classic and most impressive phenomenon to be found on a melting glacier.

Forbes did not limit his studies of glaciers to the Alps. A few years later, he brought out a companion volume, *Norway and Its Glaciers, Visited in 1851.* He did, however, dedicate his first volume to Johann Wolfgang von Goethe (1749–1832) with the words "*Sage mir was du an diesen kalten und starren Liebhabereyen gefunden hast.*" (Translation: Tell me what you have found in these cold and rigid fancies).

A massive glacier table on the lower Mer de Glace above Chamonix. Impressive features such as this seldom last more than part of one summer season before tipping over. *David Forbes.*

Professor Forbes, who also became known to subsequent generations of those who studied glaciers because of his particular concern with the origin of the "dirt band" features of many retreating glaciers' ablation zones, took further note of the phenomenon of glacier tables on page 25 of the aforementioned book, with an eloquent description of such a feature: "Some block, of greater size than its neighbours, covering a considerable surface of the ice, becomes detached from them, and seems shot up upon an icy pedestal." Such large rocks, particularly if flatter and of an optimum thickness, provide shade from the actinic rays that melt the surrounding icy surface, thereby protecting that which is immediately beneath and, with time, thus appearing to rise above the general surface of the glacier. Eight pages further, he notes (in precise but more poetic language) that:

> The glacier moves on, like the river, with a steady flow, though no eye sees its motion; but from day to day, and from year to year, the secret, silent cause produces the certain, slow effect; the avalanche feeds it, and swells its flowing tide; the mightiest masses which lightning, or the elements, roll down from the mountainside upon its surface, are borne along

> without pause; when the glacier, advancing beyond its usual limit, presses forward into the lower valleys, it turns up the soil, and wrinkles, far in advance, the greensward of the meadows, with its tremendous plowshare; it brings amongst the fields the blasts of winter, and overthrows trees and houses like stubble in its ruthless progress …
>
> The first person, so far as I know, who perceived the possible importance of glaciers as geological agents, was my respected predecessor, Professor Playfair[1] [in his book *Illustrations of the Huttonina Theory of the Earth*].
>
> "For the moving of large masses of rock," says Professor Playfair, "the most powerful agents without doubt which nature employs are the glaciers, those lakes and rivers of ice which are formed in the highest valleys of the Alps, and other mountains of the first order. These great masses are in perpetual motion, undermined by the influx of heat[2] from the earth, and impelled down the declivities on which they rest, by their enormous weight, together with that of the innumerable fragments of rock with which they are loaded. These fragments they gradually transport to their utmost boundaries, where a formidable wall ascertains the magnitude, and attest the force, of the great engine by which it was erected."

Forbes is discussing here the unsorted mineral material that would be termed either a terminal or a recessional moraine, such as forms the dams for countless well-known alpine lakes — including, but definitely not limited to: Lake Louise, the Lago di Garda, Loch Ness, Lake Geneva, the Finger Lakes of upstate New York, the diminutive Slide Lake near the Continental Divide in Colorado, and the even tinier Hermit Lake in Mount Washington's Tuckerman Ravine.

Forbes went on (on page 43) to touch on the field of research into the written (and oral) history of Alpine areas — a topic more fully developed in later years by the expatriate American clergyman and scholar William Augustus Brevoort Coolidge (1850–1926), who edited the *Alpine Journal* for many years and lies buried in the east churchyard at Grindelwald. His delayed cultural impact is referenced in many subsequent scholarly works.

Thus, it is not out of place to recount here one of the most touching Swiss legends, recorded by the Reverend Coolidge (as viewed by the author in a manuscript at the Grindelwald church where Coolidge is buried):

> Saint Theodule was bishop of the Valais in the years prior to 381 AD and found that his cathedral at Martigny was subject to frequent "jökulhlaup"

> floods from the Dranse River (which joins the Rhone at this place). Since the Devil had caused the floods that damaged Martigny, to avoid further conflict, Theodule decided to relocate his episcopal seat eastward to the city of Sion, and everyone pitched in to build the new church. But, because there was no suitable foundry in the Valais, upon its completion, Theodule had no bell for his fine new cathedral, and decided to go to Rome to ask Pope Damasus (regnant 366–384) for help.
>
> The pope was prompt in finding a suitable bell, but Theodule then had to face the now daunting and critical issue of how to get his big, new bell from Rome across the main chain of the Alps to Sion. At this point, Satan appeared, anxious as always to garner a soul for his kingdom (particularly one as holy as that of Theodule), and offered the bishop a deal: He would transport the saint, all his equipage, and the new bell to Sion, overnight, IF, Theodule would surrender his soul to the Devil. After pondering all the considerations of this difficult offer, the saint accepted; provided however, that the Devil would guarantee to get the entire job done before dawn, so that his parishioners would not be scandalized by seeing him consorting with the 'Prince of Darkness.' Satan agreed to this stipulation and thereupon gathered the saint, his mule and the new bell into his enormous satchel and headed north. But, he opted not to take the usual route over the Great Saint Bernard Pass, utilizing instead the glacier pass just east of the Matterhorn, a higher but more direct line from Rome to Sion.
>
> Faced, therefore, with the stiff upgrade from Breuil, the Devil got behind schedule as the night wore on, and light was appearing in the eastern sky when he arrived with his load in the churchyard of Sion, at which precise moment St. Theodule's rooster announced the dawn — and the Devil was deprived of his payment. That high pass, however, at more than 11,000 feet, still bears the name of Theodule.

Forbes, who had momentarily overlooked the glacial sculpting of the braes and bens of his homeland, also cited one of his near contemporary scientists, Ignaz Venetz (1788–1859), the cantonal engineer of the Valais, who had first come to wider notice because of his strenuous (but ultimately futile) attempts to avert yet another jökulhlaup [glacial outburst flood] in the lower valley of the Dranse, upstream from Martigny.

> M. Venetz, an intelligent engineer of the canton of Valais, speculating on the irregular periods of increase and decrease of glaciers, collected partly

*Left:* Cathedral of Sion, complete with bell, and now safe from the jökulhlaups of the Dranse. According to legend, this greensward was the landing spot of the Devil and St. Theodule — overnight from Rome and one cock crow too late. *W. L. Putnam III.*

*Below:* The massive dam in Val de Bagnes, upstream from Martigny, built in 1931. So far this has prevented further downstream jökulhlaups while providing the "head" for generating electric power. *W. L. Putnam III.*

> from history and partly from tradition, a variety of curious and distinct facts bearing on these oscillations of the great glaciers of the Alps. He united them with judgment and impartiality in a memoir which was read in 1821 to the Swiss Natural History Society [La Société Helvétique des Sciences Naturelles] and published in the second part of their Transactions. In this paper, M. Venetz classifies separately the facts which prove an increase, and those showing a decrease in modern times. The former are certainly the most remarkable — showing that passes the most inaccessible, traversed now perhaps but once in twenty years, were frequently passed on foot, sometimes traversed on horseback, between the twelfth and fifteenth centuries. Thus the Protestants of the Haut Valais took their children across what is now the Great Glacier of Aletsch to Grindelwald for baptism, and at the same period horses passed [over] the Monte Moro from Saas [Fe] into Italy.

Venetz's paper was read in 1821 and contains a number of scholarly references to the classics, particularly the writings of Virgil, but was not published for

The longest glacier in the Alps, the Aletsch, flows south from the Jungfrau, the Eiger (partially clouded), and the Mönch, via the Konkordiaplatz. Its meltwater drains to the Rhone River after gathering most of the precipitation from the famed Bernese Oberland peaks. Shown here in 2013 from a stance above its lateral moraine, the unweathered freshness of the exposed area above today's ice shows how greatly reduced the Aletsch is from the recent past. *W. L. Putnam III.*

another dozen years, during which period other budding scientists, such as Forbes and Agassiz, made the scientific headlines involving glaciation. The critical section of Venetz's work comes just after he cites Virgil[3] in his first book of *Géorgics*: "Take care to learn of time, the winds, and habits of the heavens …" Early in this noteworthy paper, Venetz wrote the critical lines that justify the merit in much scientific inquiry that may be secondary in method to the direct inspection of the ultimately desired data: *"A défaut des observations thermometriques, on doit recourir à des moyen par lesquels on pourra approximativement juger de l'état de la temperature des temps reculés."* Translation: In the absence of [direct] thermometric observations, one must resort to means by which one can roughly gauge the state of the temperature in ancient times.

• • •

The process of moving "large masses of rock," as noted by Professor Playfair, was discussed by Forbes on page 48 in the following paragraph:

> Upon the slope of this range [the Jura], — not at the level of the lake [Neuchâtel] but considerably higher, and just facing the Rhone valley, lie extensive deposits of angular blocks of the kind of granite which especially characterizes the eastern part of the Range of Mont Blanc, which is also the nearest point where the rock in question occurs *in situ*. It may be difficult to point out with certainty the locality whence these fragments are derived, as the kind of granite called Protogene[4] (which contains talc instead of mica) of which they consist, is common in many parts of the Alps. But it is perfectly certain that no [bed]rock approaching it in the remotest degree is to be found in the Jura, or nearer than the part of the Alps which I have mentioned, and which may be from 60 to 70 miles [100± kilometers] distant as the crow flies. A great belt of these rocks occupies a line, extending for miles, at an average height of 800 feet above the level of the Lake of Neuchâtel, and above and below that line, they diminish in number, although not entirely wanting. They have been most extensively broken up and removed, for building purposes, or merely to disencumber the land, and many have been concealed amidst the woods which clothe the mountain slope. But wherever seen they fill the mind with astonishment, when it is recollected that, as a matter of certainty, these vast rocks, larger than no mean cottages, have been removed from the distant peaks of the Alps, visible in dim perspective amidst their eternal snows.

Scientists should not necessarily be compared to poets and philosophers; however, Professor Forbes, in his concluding passages (p. 386) wrote:

> Poets and philosophers have delighted to compare the course of human life to that of a river; perhaps a still apter simile might be found in the history of a [mountain] glacier. Heaven-descended in its origin, it yet takes its mould and conformation from the hidden womb of the mountains which brought it forth. At first soft and ductile, it acquires a character and firmness of its own, as an inevitable destiny urges it on its onward career. Jostled and constrained by the crosses and inequalities of its prescribed path, hedged in by impassable barriers which fix limits to its movements, it yields groaning to its fate, and still travels forward, seamed with the scars of many a conflict with opposing obstacles. All this while, although wasting, it is renewed by an unseen power, — it evaporates, but is not consumed.

• • •

In the days before man began to utilize scientific methods of study, mythology, fear, and religion appear to have dominated the thinking of the curious. Thus, we find data on religious involvement with the dreadful advances of mountain glaciers coming from a biography of Jean d'Arathon d'Alex[5] (1620–1695), who was the Roman Catholic bishop of Geneva (mostly in absentia, thanks to John Calvin and his successors) from 1660 until his death. In this two-volume biography, republished at Lyon in 1834, one can read (en français, as translated by the noted English engraver/alpinist, Edward Whymper) of an event that took place in 1690:

> The inhabitants of a parish called Chamounix shewed in a remarkable manner the confidence they put in the blessing of their bishop. Chamounix is upon the frontiers of the Valais, having great mountains laden with snow and ice in summer as well as in winter; their height seems to carry their tops to the skies, and they rise almost as far as the sight can reach; and the snow and ice, continually inclining downwards, threaten to ruin the surrounding localities. Whenever the Bishop visited this region, the people begged him to exorcise and bless these icy mountains. About five years before his death, they sent him a deputation to beg him to come once more, offering to pay his expenses, and assuring him that since his last visit, the glaciers had retreated more than eighty paces. The Bishop,

delighted at their faith, replied, "Yes, my good friends, I will come to add my prayers to yours."

"I have a declaration," says one writer, "made on oath before the most notable persons of those parts, in which it is sworn that since this benediction by Jean d'Arathon, the glaciers have retreated, to such an extent that they are now an eighth of a league from the places where they were formerly."

• • •

In the first volume of *Peaks, Passes, and Glaciers,* published in 1858, one can also read (starting on page 400, as chapter XVI) an article titled "The Old Glaciers of Switzerland and North Wales" by Sir Andrew Crombie Ramsay[6]:

> It is now twenty years since Agassiz and Buckland announced that the valleys of the Highlands and of Wales had once been filled with glaciers. Few but geologists heard the announcement, and, with rare exceptions, those who cared at all about it met the glacial theory of the Drift in general, and that of extinct glaciers in particular, with incredulity and sometimes with derision. Rash writers still held that the far-borne boulder drift, so widely spread over the cold and temperate regions of Europe, Asia and America, had been scattered abroad by mighty sea waves, set in motion by the sudden upheaval of hypothetical northern continents; and the polish and striation of the rocks in mountain valleys — the veritable signs of vanished glaciers — were attributed by flippant writers and talkers, to cart wheels, hob-nailed boots, and the nether integuments of Welshmen sliding down the hills; as if the country had been inhabited by a monstrous race of primitive Celts — all clad in the famous armour of stone worn by Loupgarou and his giants, when they fought against the heroic Pantagruel [Legendary werewolves and giants of Celtic folklore]. — their sole occupation for illimitable ages having consisted in the performance of Titanic glissades upon the rocks.
>
> But now the tide has changed, and for years the glacial theory (applied to a late Tertiary epoch in Britain and elsewhere) has not only steadily gained ground among geologists, but has even found its way into the writings of popular authors [e.g., Jonathan Swift[7]]. I now propose to show briefly, as far as my data will permit, the relation of these extinct glaciers to those of Switzerland, and of both to the erratic Drift that often covers the lowlands.

Swiss naturalist Johann Jakob Scheuchzer (1672–1733) sketched a variety of interesting, if imaginative, things that he "encountered" in his travels around the Alps. *Johann Jakob Scheuchzer.*

William Buckland (1784–1856), one of the many unrecorded transitory figures between religion-dominated folklore and reality-based learning, attempted to bring a measure of agreement between literalist clergymen and reality — bridging evolving scientific knowledge and Biblical literalism. Having received Holy Orders, he became a pioneering professor of geology at Oxford while continuing to also deny any merit in the concept of evolution. On the other hand, Ramsay bridged that tradition-generated gap with ease (and did it quite well) in the many pages of his works that ensued.

Climate change — as manifested by the retreat of mountain glaciers, is not merely a record of melting ice when things get warm but may well be more of a record of altered precipitation in the upland (accumulation) zones of a glacier. Thus, we cite a somewhat different story of glacial comings and goings in the Saint Elias Range, home of North America's most massive present ice sheet. The United States Geological Survey Professional Paper 1616: "A Geologic Guide to the Wrangell-Saint Elias National Park and Preserve, Alaska" (ISBN 0-607-92676-7), prepared by Gary R. Winkler in 2000, is a comprehensive analysis of both the ancient bedrock and the more modern glaciers in the area between Copper River and Glacier Bay — including the apparently contradictory melting back of the glaciers feeding into Icy Bay and the concurrent advance of those just a short distance away:

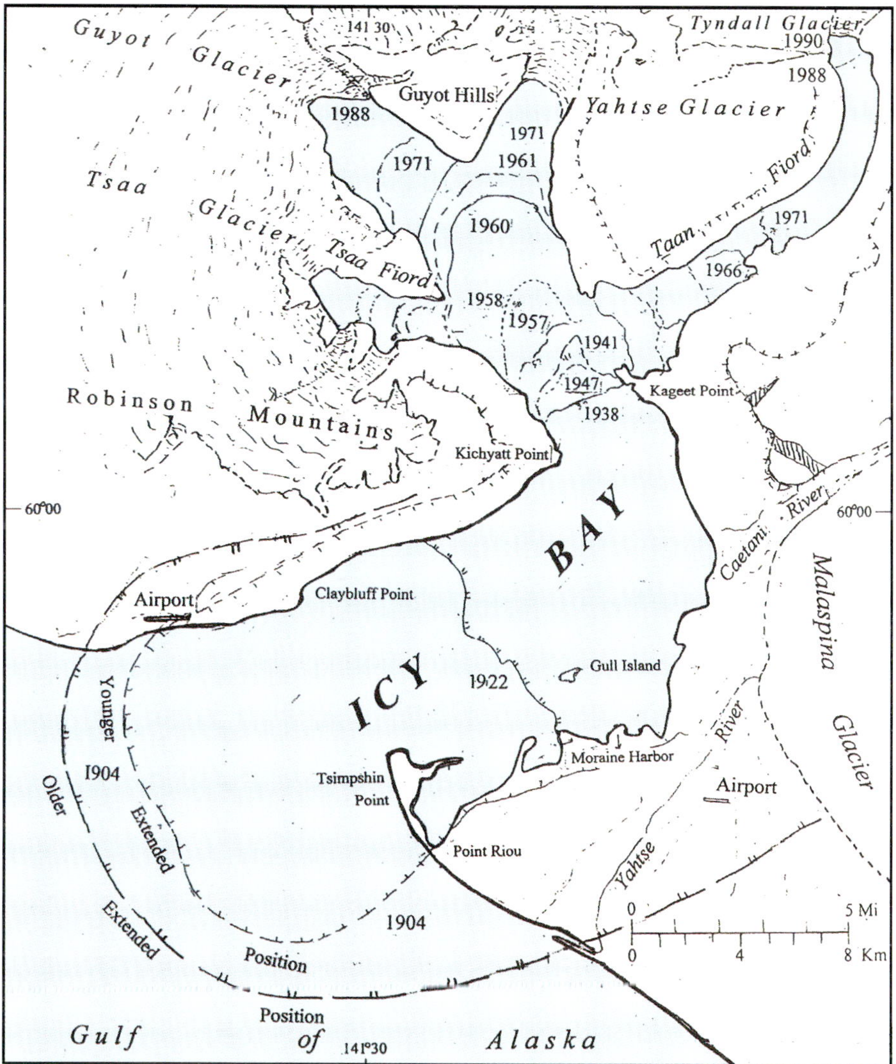


Austin Stuart Post (1922–2012), Alaska's premier glaciologist, created this map of the glacier termini in Icy Bay, at the westerly edge of the great Malaspina Glacier, in his Open File Report 83-256. In 1946, this scribe and his seven companions marched for three strenuous days from near Kageet Point northeastward to the farthest point shown on this map. Our Camp VII (toward Mount Saint Elias) was made over what was then the rock-strewn, heavily crevassed, and two-mile-wide Tyndall Glacier and is now Taan Fiord, accessible over its more than ten-mile length by sea kayak. *Austin Stuart Post.*

> Extending nearly across the mouth of Yakutat Bay [in coastal Alaska] is a submerged moraine complex, deposited during the maximum advance of Hubbard Glacier[8] (or, more properly, the Yakutat — Disenchantment Bay lobe of the combined Malaspina and Hubbard Glaciers) sometime between about 1,000 and 700 years ago. Thus, Hubbard Glacier has retreated nearly 40 mi northeastward in the last several hundred years to expose Yakutat and Disenchantment Bays. Even so, Hubbard is North America's largest tidewater glacier, and has a face nearly 6 mi wide that reaches heights of close to 300 feet. Ice retreat began sometime before 1400 and proceeded slowly but steadily for several centuries.
>
> A submerged moraine at the west end of Disenchantment Bay resulted from a temporary readvance that culminated between 1700 and 1791. At the time of explorer Malaspina's search for the fabled Northwest Passage [in 1792] he navigated Yakutat Bay without difficulty, but was turned back in the vicinity of Haenke Island by floating ice that was impenetrable to his vessels. The name he gave to the fiord at the head of Yakutat Bay, 'Desengaña,' indicates his disenchantment that no passage existed. Between 1792 and 1894, the terminus of Hubbard Glacier resumed its retreat to a position about 2 mi east of its current location near Osier Island. Since 1894, when systematic mapping of its terminus began, Hubbard Glacier has slowly readvanced, threatening to seal the mouth of Russell Fiord. In early 1986, the threat came true; Hubbard Glacier advanced sufficiently to block the connection between Disenchantment Bay and Russell Fiord. The water behind the glacial dam began to rise, creating a temporary 'Lake Russell.' In the 5 months that the dam held, the lake rose about 82 feet above sea level, but in early October, 1986, the dam failed and the lake emptied completely within the course of 28–30 hours. A new closure will likely take place in the near future unless Hubbard Glacier's slow advance is stabilized or reversed.

The Hubbard Glacier has long been nearly unique in its terminal configuration in that it bifurcated at Osier Island (as did the glacier once occupying today's Lago di Como in Italy at Bellagio) with one branch, Russell Fiord, going more southeastward and providing a large terminal outwash delta some distance east-southeast of Yakutat, and the other branch advancing more directly toward modern Yakutat, as described above.

One of the more complete chronologies (within locally historic times) of glacial comings and goings is that pertaining to Icy Bay, Alaska — the next indentation west, up the coast, from Yakutat — that was formulated by Austin Stuart Post, Alaskan glaciologist extraordinaire, who attached the map [p. 47] to his Open File Report 83–256. This map clearly documents the local effects of recent centuries of global warming. The Tsaa, Guyot, and Yahtse Glaciers are completely "low level" (that is, higher temperature) operations, as is much of the catchment area of the closely adjacent Tyndall Glacier. Whereas, by contrast, the main catchment area pertinent to the recently surging Hubbard Glacier is considerably farther inland, more "continental," and much higher above sea level. It is, therefore, cooler, and the precipitation is more likely to be in the form of snow, not rain.

*Better suffer for truth than*
*prosper by falsehood*

— Danish proverb

Swiss Alps

IV

# Peaks, Passes, and Glaciers

*by Members of the Alpine Club*

The Alpine Club, an exclusive, male-only, and mostly English society, was founded on December 22, 1857, at a dinner hosted by Edward Shirley Kennedy[1] in a private dining room at Ashley's Hotel on Norfolk Park in London, to which had been invited a number of those gentlemen who had been accustomed to making recreational visits to the major mountain ranges of Western Europe. (Women were not allowed to join, so they consequently founded the Ladies Alpine Club some fifty years later. However, this sexist bylaw was eliminated by economic necessity in 1975 when it was belatedly recognized that the wives tended to outlive their husbands and were thus able to leave far more to their club than had their spouses, and the two clubs merged at last.) While its membership was deliberately limited to those who had already demonstrated proficiency at traveling through and onto these mountains, the club's members were not snobbish in recording data of general interest to others. Thus, the club's first publication, the following year (1858), opens with the words: "In presenting this volume to the public ..."

Thereafter followed three additional volumes of *Peaks, Passes, and Glaciers*, and in 1864, the first volume of the club's annual Journal, and has been published with scholarly regularity ever since,[2] as the club's membership grew and its members found their way into mountain areas around the world. The English example was soon followed in other countries of Europe, where alpine societies — all more plebeian in their membership — soon became significantly larger than the English original. In 1876, this process reached across the Atlantic Ocean to Boston with the founding of the MIT-dominated Appalachian Mountain Club. Later, it reached the Far East (by way of New Zealand in 1891) with the establishment of the Japanese Alpine Club in 1905.

In its journal, the club's members reported events of significance to mountaineers — avalanche dangers, mountain forest denudation, new ascents, evolving mountain amenities, and the tribulations of mountain glaciers, then to be found in abundance in the major valleys of almost all elevated regions of the world but nowadays approaching the status of a dwindling rarity. However, even those who are not concerned — or do not care to be bothered or informed about — the cause of this melting, don't have to look very far to see where all that meltwater has gone. The residents of seaside homes — from the Fiji and Maldive Islands to coastal New Jersey and Long Island — already have a fair idea. But worse is sure to come, for glaciologists estimate that when interior Greenland becomes totally ice-free (as it seems to have been in the distant past), sea levels will rise worldwide by eight to ten feet, and an ice-free Antarctica (where the bedrock has numerous fossils) could deliver more than eighty feet more.

Climatological studies, such as one widely reported in late 2013 by scientists from the university of Hawaii, have concentrated on the warming effect of man's incessant pollution of Earth's atmosphere, but the equally likely rise of sea levels is even scarier. This process will assuredly drown out every major and capital city of the modern world — with the interesting exceptions of Beijing, Chicago, and Moscow. And since most of the world's population lives at altitudes at or below 100 feet above sea level, looking at the issue homogenically, where will all these billions of people go?

The wasting away of mountain glaciers has been documented in many of the journals of alpine societies. Initially, in the mid-nineteenth century, these reports dealt with glacial advances and retreats — as observed by alpinists from year to year. But as time went on, and surely by the mid-twentieth century, the global trend became impossible to ignore. Living conditions for mountain glaciers were fast becoming very difficult indeed. (See Appendix of Comparisons for a pictorial exposition of this matter.)

Indicating yet another but opposite climatic "switcheroo," less than a mile from the stance where the comparison pictures of the Sir Sandford Glacier were taken, David Peter Jones came across inland cedar tree stumps half-buried by rocky debris that had fallen from above, but several hundred feet above the valley bottom, on the northern, sunnier side of an area that Howard Palmer had called the "Silvertip Névé" — later renamed the Hayworth Glacier. In a private communication (to this scribe) Jones wrote:

> The GSC [Geological Survey of Canada] dated [by $C_{14}$ analysis] my samples (#6772) at 3870, ± 60 years, BP[3] [ca. 1860 BCE]. Given the size of

these cedar stumps and their location indicates that the tree line was well above this location (inland cedars do not usually grow at or near tree line). While I do not have a precise number, I would guess that tree line was probably 500m. or more higher than this location. The other implication is that there were probably few (if any) glaciers in the Selkirks at such time, and those that existed were probably small and well up in headwall cirques.

a) Palisade Ridge and Hayworth Glacier, 2010. *David P. Jones.*

b) Stump and Silvertip Glacier, 2010. *David P. Jones.*

c) Stump of an inland cedar tree that was a seedling about 1860 BCE. Note the active glacier in the background (b) and the ice axe for comparison; it was a big tree. *David P. Jones.*

Not far away, only 20 miles [30 kilometers] to the south of the waning Sir Sandford Glacier, lies the town and station of Glacier on the Canadian Pacific Railway. When the place was named in 1883, the "great" Illecillewaet Glacier[4] swept down from its 9,000-foot catchment area to the south and was such a prominent feature that the railway then named its hotel and dining stop the Glacier House.[5] So noteworthy was this spectacular glacier that it was seized on in 1887 by the members of the Vaux family of Philadelphia — Mary, George Jr., and William Jr., among the world's pioneer glaciologists — as the site for their initial studies of glacier motion, wastage, and retreat. A dozen years later, they presented their first comprehensive report on it to the Philadelphia Academy of Natural Sciences:

> The source of the glacier is in the great snow field or névé which covers the comparatively level portions of the higher mountain ranges. By the action of the Sun and pressure, this snow is very much compressed, till the crystals are frozen together and form clear ice. It is at this point that the glacier proper begins.
>
> Whilst ice cannot be made to flow like water as we consider it in the ordinary sense, yet when subjected to great pressure its action is almost similar. There is a constant yielding to pressure which permits the gradual flow of glaciers, and exactly as in a river, the flow is more rapid in the center than at the sides, and on the surface than at the bottom.
>
> As the ice descends over the rough, rocky bed it becomes cracked and split into long tongues, or perhaps pinnacles, if the cracks happen to cross each other. The long fissures are called crevasses, the pinnacles, seracs. The water melted from the ice finds its way through the crevasses and wells to the bed of boulders below and passes to the outside air. Often very beautiful arches of ice are formed where the principal streams flow out. The earth and boulders which are carried down on the ice collect in moraines at the foot of the glaciers. Sometimes these piles are hundreds of feet in height.

The Glacier House is, as of 2014, long gone. (It was offered gratis to the railway's imported Swiss guides in 1915, who refused it. Then it was torn down in 1927.) Tunnels easing the often snow-covered 4 percent grade in the Rockies and under the even snowier crest of the Selkirk Range (along with diesel-electric engines and welded steel rails) have eliminated much expense and numerous fatalities and have generally speeded up railroad operations. Gone too is much of the Illecillewaet Glacier, as global warming, since it was first sighted by Major

Albert Rogers in 1883, has almost completely removed this 3,500-foot cascading paragon of Canadian alpine beauty and romantic history. However, we offer two comparison pictures in the appendix.

This is not the only example in North America of dramatic climatic warming within locally historic time. The Glacier House was located in Glacier National Park, established by Parliament in 1886 at the request of the Canadian Pacific Railway, and with good luck, one can still catch a glimpse of an actual glacier from places along its tracks through the Selkirk Range. However, in most of Alaska's Glacier Bay National Park, established in 1925 as a national monument, one can scarcely see even a remnant of glacial ice. And in the northernmost part of western Montana and adjacent parts of Alberta, the joint National Parks of Glacier Lake (initially established in 1910 at the request of the Great Northern Railroad) and Glacier-Waterton Lakes, despite what their tourist brochures show, are almost completely free of permanent snow or ice.

• • •

In an article entitled "On the Recent Retreat of the Lower Grindelwald Glacier, with Some Remarks on Other Similar Oscillations during Modern Times" (*Alpine Journal*, Vol. VI, p. 30, AUG 1872), Francis Fox Tuckett[6] wrote:

> In the church[7] at Grindelwald there is still to be seen a small bell, weighing about sixty pounds, bearing on its upper moulding the inscription, "O! Sancta Petronella, Ora pro Nobis," and on the lower, the date 1044, with wide but regular intervals between the figures. It is believed that the inhabitants of this district were first converted to Christianity in the tenth or, at earliest, in the ninth century, and it is believed that the bell in question originally belonged to a chapel dedicated to St. Petronella,[8] which was erected in a cave still accessible, and situated near what was at that time the end of the Lower [Grindelwald] Glacier, and on its left, or west, bank. It is added that this chapel, and a similar one at Viesch in the Valais, marked the beginning and the end of a frequented pass across the ridge of the Viescherhörner, or Walcherhörner, as they were formerly called. No less general is the belief that on several occasions, and amongst others in 1578, children have been brought over this high pass to be baptised at Grindelwald with the Protestant rite.

In this medieval period, there appeared to have been considerable traffic across

(a) The bell of Saint Petronella is still found in the old church at Grindelwald, but it is no longer on public display. *W. L. Putnam III.*

(b) The Gold Mine Adit at Borca in the Val Anzasca is now a tourist attraction, but much of the gold used in Renaissance art and by the Papacy came from this and other mines in the extensive Pre-Cambrian schist formations of this area. *W. L. Putnam III.*

(c) The town square of Macugnaga in the Anzasca Valley south of the Monte Moro is nestled in the afternoon shadow of the 15,203-meter-high Monte Rosa, the second highest point of the Alps. The highest crest of this peak, the Dufourspitze, is named for Guillaume-Henri Dufour (1787–1875), the Swiss general who presided over the First Geneva Conference in 1864. Note the Yäger Bar. *W. L. Putnam III.*

the higher Alpine passes from one linguistic and cultural zone to another as well as for religious purposes. The passage from German-speaking Saas-Fee over the 2,868-meter Monte Moro Pass into the Italian-speaking and famously auriferous Anzasca Valley[9] was crossed by laden horses repeatedly into the seventeenth century. This process has resulted in the incongruous name for one of this scribe's favorite watering holes — Bar Burgener in the Staffa section of Macugnaga, along with several other nomenclative anomalies. Tuckett then went on with a lengthy passage citing some other church records and concluded:

> It is no doubt true that at a former period the direct intercourse between the Oberland and the Valais was much more frequent than at present, but communication via the Vieschergrat must be relegated to the mythic period rather than sought for in the sixteenth century. It appears to be proved that in the year 1712, on the outbreak of the last Swiss war of religion,[10] some Protestants of the Valais fled across the glaciers to Grindelwald; but it is stated that it was at the cost of great labour and hardship, and that the party reached Grindelwald in a half-dead condition.

At the time of this scribe's most recent visit to Grindelwald, the shrine dedicated to Petronella was no longer known even to the operators of a hotel near where it had been. The "schlucht" beneath the Lower Grindelwald Glacier, referred to by Tuckett, aided by the rock flour accompanying the frigid meltwater, had widened the gorge dramatically from the time of the scribe's last visit and enabled the construction of a walkway for tourists along the left side of the stream (complete with bungee-jumping platform for a 280-meter ride to the river's edge).

In the *Alpine Journal*, Vol. VII, for February of 1875, one of its longest-lived and most erudite editors, Douglas William Freshfield (1845–1934) — who had been introduced to alpinism by his mother and became one of the most distinguished geographers and alpinists of all time — wrote, on page 267, under "Alpine Notes":

> When visiting the Hüfi glacier [in Canton Uri of central Switzerland] I found it has retreated very considerably. This regression has, it seems, been going on for three years. Professor A. Heim[11] states in Vol IX of the Swiss Jahrbuch, that during the 26 months between August, 1871, and November, 1873, the glacier retreated 486 feet. This continued in winter as well as in summer. Between November 3, 1871, and May 28, 1872, it retreated 30 feet; between November 24, 1872 and 25 May, 1873, no

The one-time bed of the Hüfi Glacier as seen from the height of the Grimsel pass in 2003. *W. L. Putnam III.*

> less than 110 feet. In the ten days following May 28, 1872, it advanced 1 foot, but in the following 39 days it retreated 77 feet.

The term "retreat," as used by Freshfield above with reference to a glacier, does *not* mean that the body of ice moved backward up the valley; rather than the melting at its snout, it exceeded the slow forward motion of the moving ice. The subject of glacial recession drew continuous interest and comment from club members as noted August 1877 (*Alpine Journal*, Vol. VIII, p. 275) by Charles Marret:

> Mr. F. F. Tuckett, in the sixth vol. of the 'Alpine Journal,' p. 30 [above] has given an exceedingly interesting account of the retreat of the Lower Grindelwald Glacier, and of the uncovering of ancient marble quarries from beneath it. He also gives reasons for believing that the glaciers were at a minimum about the year 1750; that between that time and 1771 they had rapidly increased, and had not again diminished until after 1850, since which time the retreat has been continuous and very remarkable. Up to about that time the glaciers were no doubt increasing and the Swiss expressed some anxiety on the subject. Soon afterwards the advance

The Lower Grindelwald Glacier (a), referred to in the text, no longer enters the "schlucht" (b) inferred by Tuckett. Its meltwater stream is spanned by a sturdy masonry arch (c) connecting the Hotel Gletscherschlucht to the town. The "schlucht" itself now has a passageway hacked into the solid limestone that extends almost half its length. *W. L. Putnam III.*

> ceased, and in many of them a retreat began; not, however, in all of them, for the Findelen Glacier at Zermatt was, in 1859, encroaching on the pastures and turning up old turf like a gigantic ploughshare. The natives give us a reason for the retreat, an unusual number of mild winters, and most of the old Swiss travelers will say that the summers have on the whole been hotter and finer than they were formerly. The inhabitants of Chamonix declare that their crops ripen a fortnight earlier, and attribute this to the diminution of the glaciers[12]: more, however, is probably due to the warm summers and to improved cultivation.
>
> I have made no actual observations, but as I was at Chamonix and at Grindelwald in 1830 and 1831, at Grindelwald again in 1852, at Chamonix again in 1854, and at both again in 1875, I am perhaps able to form a tolerable estimate of the vast changes of which the younger generation of tourists can have no notion. I find, moreover, that my rough estimate agrees very exactly with the estimates formed by the Swiss engineers from careful measurements and continued observations.
>
> My recollections of 1830 and 1831 were in 1852 and 1854 tolerably distinct, and I am sure that I saw no remarkable changes when I visited the glaciers. The change in 1875 was so great that I can best give the younger readers of the Journal a notion by saying that the difference is as much as that between the Thames opposite Greenwich at high water, and the same at low water …
>
> The Lower Glacier of Grindelwald, which formerly projected into the valley, has fallen back at least a quarter of a mile, leaving some bare rocks and a large irregular piece of ground covered with stones and rubbish. The front is now well within the line of the Mettenhorn and Eiger, and the celebrated pinnacles of ice which were formed by the pressure in that narrow space have all vanished. There is now (1875) merely a dirty front, or rather tongue, of smooth ice, deeply crevassed, coming down to the plain and just filling the narrow space between the mountains. The deep scores in the rocks above, show how great the pressure used to be. The glacier has also sunk at least 300 feet. The stream from it is now seen flowing through a deep ravine or cleft in the rocks [schlucht] which was until of late years buried under the glacier and invisible. It is to this glacier that the very interesting paper by Mr. F. F. Tuckett … relates.

By way of support for the universality of the conditions expressed by Tuckett, two years later [Vol. IX; p. 241ff], James Eccles[13] wrote concerning an interesting

Wind River Peak shows its glacial sculpting well in this view from the south. *American Alpine Club.*

observation he made while reporting on the first climbs done in the Wind River Range of Wyoming — a long way from the Alps but of similar latitude and elevation. Fortunately for Eccles, he had made the acquaintance of Frederick Vandeveer Hayden (1829–1887), then in the process of establishing the United States Geological Survey. Through Hayden's good offices, Eccles and his guide were permitted to join a USGS field party led by Allen David Wilson (1844–1920), later the USGS Chief of Cartography charged with the topographical surveys of western Wyoming in the summer of 1878. The following passage concerns events that occurred in July after they had climbed the Wind River Peak, the highest point they could find near their camp, and — at 13,192 feet (4,022 meters) — one of the higher points of the lower forty-eight United States:

> Instead of rejoining our companions, Michel and I struck out on a different route towards camp, passing over an intermediate summit in the hope of finding mountain sheep, and fell in with the main party on their return in the afternoon. The same evening, on ascending a hill near camp and about 1000 feet above it, I found the top covered with striae and grooves running in the direction of the lateral valley, viz. nearly north

> and south. It was clear that the glaciers on this side of the watershed had been of much greater extent than on the south-westerly side; and I had the strong suspicion, which I had not time to verify, that the glaciers on the north-east side of the range, being piled up to a higher level than the col over which we had passed, for a time overflowed through it to the west. This would be a precisely similar case to that of the ancient OberAar [Hüfi] Glacier, when it passed over the watershed above the Grimsel, and overflowed into the Rhone Valley.

• • •

Before concluding with early members of the Alpine Club, it is appropriate to note the work of Captain Marshall Hall, a gentleman-magistrate of Wiltshire, who successfully urged the club to establish a committee (William Martin Conway, Lord Allington, Professor Thomas George Bonney, and himself)[14] to study "the oscillations of the glaciers in different parts of the British Empire." In his seminal article of 1879 [*Alpine Journal*, Vol. XV, p. 348ff] he noted:

> But as to the numerous glaciers in British territory — the Himalayas, those of New Zealand, the western portions of our American possessions — if there be any records on the subject, I am unaware how to lay my hands on such.
>
> Probably no connected accounts exist. Our colonists, our military, naval and civil officers, men of science, travelers, Alpine Clubs — all seem to have joined in sublime indifference as to the history of glacial movements, and their increase or decrease, at least outside "the playground of Europe."
>
> This is all the more surprising [in] that English savants have borne so notable a part in investigations of the causes of ice-movement, whilst to our many geologists the sculpture of mountains, more or less of lakes, climate, fauna and flora are all matters in which glacial history is eminently important …
>
> The task of correlating individual observations and reports would be reduced easily to a minimum if such a committee, inviting the assistance of men in various countries, would arrange a code, so to speak, to be adhered to by all who could be induced to adopt it.
>
> I am too much of a cosmopolitan, I confess, to care greatly where the domicile of origin of such a code might be. But since The Alpine Club

> is admittedly the senior body of its kind, we should like to see that, after coming to the front, it also makes an early advance to the attack.
>
> Our members, after ascending all the 'inaccessible' peaks, are now ranging themselves into two bodies of climbers — some of us strenuously determined to find what I may call all the wrong ways up the old peaks, the others exploring the great ranges the world over.

On this very theme, when this scribe was considerably younger, it was the unpublished "duty" of all serious alpinists in the United States to photograph the snouts of any glaciers they might encounter with regularity — no matter where — and send all such evidence to William [Bradford] Osgood Field (1904–1994), the lifelong "glaciologist in residence" at the American Geographical Society in New York.[15] This ongoing glacier snout project came to an end during Field's final years when it was obvious to all concerned that glaciers, worldwide, were in retreat, and there was less of a need to document individual glacier performances than to determine what was at the root of this overriding global trend.

Sir George Everest was the fourth noteworthy British military engineer to head the Great Trigonometrical Survey of India, and he is surely the best known. *Royal Geographical Society.*

Hall (1831–1896), however, was apparently not a real military personage, as he seems to have been unaware of the espionage trip of 1845 by Lieutenant (later General) Henry James Warre (1819–1898) in company with the military artist, Lieutenant Mervin Vavasour (1821–1866), across the Rocky Mountains of Canada with the annual brigade of the Hudson's Bay Company. They traversed the then-unglaciated Athabaska Pass en route to the Oregon Territory to assess its military tenability in the face of American President James Knox Polk's successful election campaign slogan of "54°40′ or fight!"[16] Hall also appears to have been ignorant of the formation, in 1799, of the Great Survey of India, which had already gone through its first four leaders — the mathematician Colonel William Lambton (1753–1823), the Irish-born Colonel Valentine Blacker (1778–1826), the

Welsh-born Sir George Everest (1790–1866), and General Andrew Scott Waugh (1810–1878), many of whose often-disguised native agents had already plotted the extent of numerous glaciers in the Karakoram and Himalayas. In addition, the Royal Geographical Society had been founded in 1830, an organization whose membership with reciprocal library privileges (thanks to Freshfield) overlapped with that of the Alpine Club.

The then enormous extent of glaciers in the Himalayan and Karakoram Ranges was soon to be made more fully known to the Western world by the explorations of an American mountaineering couple, William Henry and Fanny Bullock Workman,[17] natives of Massachusetts who crossed through the Karakoram as part of a series of exploratory ventures early in the twentieth century. Then came Sven Hedin, who determined the northern limits of the Karakoram Ranges.

• • •

By the end of the nineteenth century, Alpine Club members, besides being largely of a scholarly and scientific bent, were increasingly reconciled to the facts that (1) hotel and access facilities were better than ever in the Alps; (2) the glaciers in the world's mountains (absent temporary or locally operative phenomena, such as earthquakes) seemed to be mostly in retreat; and (3) almost all routes to, or on, peaks that were initially dependent on extensive traversing of snow or glacier ice were becoming routinely more difficult or tedious than stated in the earliest guidebooks.

By the end of the twentieth century, despite their increasing use of fossil-fueled devices to aid in gaining access to remote mountain areas, serious alpinists worldwide (Alpine Club members and otherwise) were expressing nearly unanimous concern over the viability of all mountain glaciers and had almost unanimously become leaders in the burgeoning conservation movement. At this point, it is more than parenthetical to observe that the accurate recording of mountain glacier recession, and often contemporaneous thinning, has been affected in many ways as a result of occasional earthquakes. Few researchers have actually witnessed this process and have only deduced the event from distant seismic records or a later unexpected advance of certain glaciers. But at one point in the summer of 1911, Mrs. Workman and her party were camped on the Kasberi Glacier in the Karakoram when:

> At one of the most rickety, cheerless bivouacs a few miles above the tongue, at 6:30 AM, the glacier under my tent began to rock, as if the

> ice-foundations were being uprooted. I rushed from my tent, fearing the ice-hill would split and let me and my belongings into uncanny depths. They did not, but a rain of rocks and boulders composing the surface of all the surrounding hillocks was prodigious, while added to the clatter came the incessant booming of avalanches from adjacent mountains, producing such a tumult of nature as only seismic disturbances in a great, unstable mountain-region can call forth.
>
> The oscillations were sharp and short, but in that environment, accompanied by the near thunder from peaks and glacier, which continued for forty minutes, the effect on the mind was decidedly gruesome.[18]

The result of this kind of alpine "shakedown" is obviously a localized and unusual accumulation of material on the moving valley glacier, resembling the lumpy carcass of an unfortunate lesser creature as it passes through the lengthy intestinal tract of a python or boa constrictor — resulting in a later advance of the ice when this unusual and infrequent accumulation reaches the end of the glacier — only to be followed quite quickly by a compensatory melting and rapid retreat of the snout. However, a very heavy snow year in the catchment area of a glacier can bring on a very similar effect. But because of insufficient meteorological (or seismic) knowledge, it is difficult to relate that sort of cause with the ultimate effect. In any case, since the mid-nineteenth century, long-term trends of mountain glacier recession have been — in the particularly relevant words of Kirk Bryan — "worldwide and synchronous." And as recent research in the Eastern Himalayas by Japan's most vigorous contemporary senior alpinist, Dr. Tamotsu Nakamura, has made more widely known, they have been intensifying.

The fact that all but a minuscule few mountain (and other) glaciers appear to be melting away is indisputable. However, in the absence of rock-solid or legal proof, the cause of the current warming can be attributed to any of several factors, or a combination of them, the most obvious of which can definitely be assigned to the actions of man. All that snow and ice has obviously melted, regardless of how the liquidating process was initiated, and the resultant water has had to go somewhere; it has been taken out of "cold storage" and not gone off into space. But the process of glacial melting is so seemingly slow, the concurrent rise of the sea level so relatively unobvious (until some major weather event hits), and the individual human life span so short that mankind calls the process catastrophic when something suddenly appears out of the ordinary. Thus, we have difficulty comprehending the inexorable nature of globally influential events that are far beyond any form of individual's control. However, the occasional superstorm,

such as Hurricane Sandy — combined with the ever-growing press of humanity in seaside areas rapidly brings some of us back to reality, often with a very unpleasant jolt.

Humanity should try harder to listen to these messages from (our) "home," but such appears to be a process too difficult for most of us to accept. Instead, the collective policy of modern man has always been to try to build our way out of the last disaster we have inflicted on our planet, not fully appreciating what paleontologists have long known — but many supposedly educated persons apparently do not want to hear — that the fate of every other creature that has preceded *Homo sapiens* in a state of dominance on Earth has been that of (presumably) unintentionally destroying the very environment in which it has prospered. (See the words of Dr. Diamond in the final chapter.) In addition, because of our traditional haste to solve the unwanted effects of a prior "cure," we seldom take the time to give serious study to the underlying causes of many such issues — perhaps in the hope that if we ignore them long enough, they'll go away.

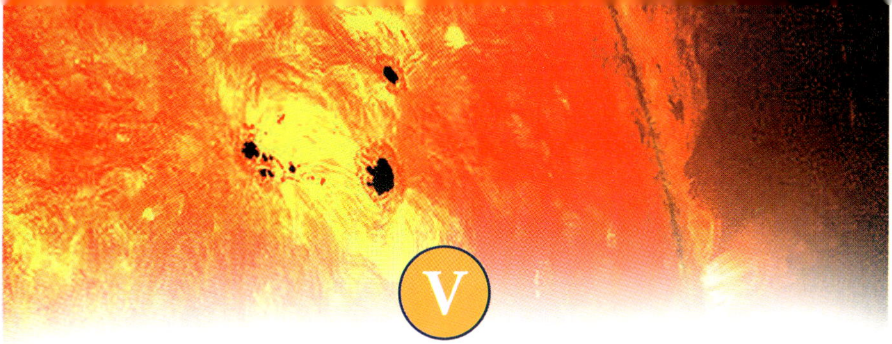

V

# Spots on the Sun

*And it shall come to pass in that day, saith the Lord GOD, that I will cause the sun to go down at noon, and I will darken the Earth on a clear day.*
— Amos 8:9 (KJB)

Edward Walter Maunder (1851–1928), the youngest son of a Wesleyan preacher, was a lifelong employee at the place where longitude begins and whence all the world's time is reckoned — the Royal Astronomical Observatory at Greenwich. Toward the close of his career, Maunder published a number of papers on sunspots, after he had observed and recorded these events for many years as the principal part of his job. (Incidentally, other nations had attempted to establish a prime meridian of their own, based on the location of their national observatories — France and the United States being the most persistent. But after publishing a few nautical and other charts in the nineteenth century that offered longitudes differing from those of the British Admiralty and finding them rejected in confusion [even by their own nationals], everyone quietly gave in to precedent and adopted Greenwich.)

Sunspots have been noted by mankind since 364 BCE; they are dark-appearing blotches that show on the rotating surface of the Sun and may last in the same solar location for several earthly days. They represent bursts of magnetic radiation and are somewhat cooler than the rest of the Sun's surface. With their current cycle of maximum appearance (about eleven earthly years), they are often visible to the unaided eye from Earth but, given the enormous speed of light and the indescribably large distances of space, still a good eight minutes after their formation.

Edward Maunder's memory rests in the timetable, or pantheon, of scientific history for having enhanced the earlier work of the nearly contemporary German astronomer, Gustav Spörer (1822–1895), who preceded him in this specialty. (Spörer's Law governs some aspects of the behavior of sunspots, and his "minimum" of sunspot appearances ran from 1420 to 1570.) Besides having redacted the reports of Galileo's first (1610) telescopic analysis of sunspots, Maunder's name has been linked to the recognition of a period of low sunspot activity (the Maunder Minimum) that extended from 1645 to 1715. This almost exactly coincided with the reign in France of Louis XIV, the Sun King of French legend, and somewhat coincided with a period that European historians have come to call the Little Ice Age, the effects of which have been noted in several other parts of the world — details follow.

While bringing all possible glory to himself, King Louis XIV of France revitalized his nation and remained the model (and often scourge) for all his contemporary rulers in western Europe. *From a picture at the Louvre.*

While the spots were inactive on the Sun, King Louis generated quite a bit of action in Western Europe, which he was only constrained from taking over completely by the great allied military cooperatives led by the English Duke of Marlborough, John Churchill (1650–1722).[1] But King Louis was sufficiently vigorous to rebuild the archaic French political and financial system as well as set a strong example of religious determinism. Scholars of Western religion will remember the Sun King for revoking the eighty-seven-year-old Edict of Nantes in 1685, which had been issued by Henri IV (of Navarre —"Paris is worth a Mass"), and which had guaranteed freedom of religion[2] to all Frenchmen. This liberal measure had long been opposed by all papal emissaries, including the regent during Louis's earlier years, Cardinal Giulio Mazarini (1602–1661), who had been elevated Prince of the Church by Galileo's nemesis, Pope Urban VIII. The revocation, however, seems largely to have been done at the request of Louis' mistress (and second queen) Madame de Maintenon. Implementation of the revocation had the almost immediate effect of flushing a lot of independent thinkers out of France, thereby benefitting the rest of Western Civilization with an influx of open-minded brainpower. (America's pioneer automakers, Charles and Frank Duryea of Springfield, Massachusetts, were of such Huguenot ancestry. Their two-cylinder horseless carriages first hit the local pavement in 1893.) All in all, that one act produced a result quite similar to Hitler's anti-Jewish pogroms of the World War II era.

• • •

The telescopic work of Galileo Galilei (1564–1642) began in 1609, and the great Pisan's troubles with the Papacy began soon after when he was "admonished" in 1616 by Pope Paul V (Camillo Borghese) to stop promoting the Copernican concept of the Sun being the central object of the solar system, as this idea differed from established Catholic dogma. Constitutionally unable to avoid discoursing to his pupils and friends on his mind-opening observations and subsequent deductions, Galileo was finally tried by the Inquisition in 1632 on the order of Pope Urban VIII (Maffeo Barberini), Paul V's twice removed successor, for this heretical teaching. Escaping torture or death, he was sentenced to spend his remaining years under congenial house arrest in Firenze, cared for by his loyal daughter, Virginia.

Galileo Galilei was undeterred by the threat of eternal damnation. This Pisan scientist publicly agreed with Copernicus and was punished for his heresy; only later was he recognized as worthy of a place in heaven. *Lowell Observatory Archives.*

Everyone knows that Galileo suffered somewhat for his scientific views — since they differed radically from the Biblical and Grecian concepts that had become Christian dogma. However, things change — even in the Church — and Pope Benedict XIV (Prospero Lorenzo Lambertini, regnant after 1740) gave the Church's imprimatur to the great Pisan's *Collected Works* in 1741.[3] It matters little, in all religious truth, what astronomical body rotates in connection with any other, but Christians of all dogmas, creeds, and sects are really no different from Buddhists,

Safely removed from papal interference (in Poland), Nikolaus Copernicus, a religious figure and pioneer of modern astronomy, demonstrated that the Sun, not the Earth, is the central item of the solar system. *Lowell Observatory Archives.*

Hindus, Muslims, Shintoists, or Sun-worshipping pagans in that what we like to believe — but cannot prove — is what we like to believe.

Mikolaj Kopernik (Copernicus, 1473–1543), who had studied at the ancient University of Bologna and became a curate at the cathedral of Frauenburg (then in East Prussia, now north Poland), had a major advantage over Galileo of not living in Italy, where one might be in more serious danger of being apprehended by the minions of a discomfited and outraged pope. Safely away from papal interruption, Copernicus worked out a system of understanding planetary motions that differed from the confusing complexity of that originated more than a thousand years earlier by Ptolemaic savants, and he was finally able to produce *De Revolutionibus Orbium Coelestium* in 1540 (dedicated to Pope Paul V), which was published after his death. Copernicus construed the solar system correctly in that the distance of each planet from the Sun is related to the diameter of its orbit. But since the less powerful instrumentation available in his day gave him no knowledge of Uranus, Neptune, and the many Kuiper Belt objects like Pluto, he can be excused for overlooking them, given what could be made out with the optics available in the early sixteenth century.

• • •

Almost all human religions are based on a lunar calendar that is slightly shorter than the solar year, but astronomers working for Julius Caesar had "annualized" the heavens and concluded that the solar year was 365.25 days in length. They then promulgated the Julian Calendar, which was thereupon implemented throughout the Roman Empire (Western Europe). By the time of Pope Gregory XIII (Ugo Boncompagni, 1502–1585), continued reliance on this calculation had escalated into a cumulative error of eleven days, for the papal savants determined that the year was actually 365 days, 5 hours, 49 minutes long — eleven minutes less than Caesar's astronomers had determined.[4] Protestant and Orthodox Christian nations were slow to adopt the resulting Gregorian Calendar. It was a Rome-induced reform, after all, and therefore suspect. For more than a century, many historical accounts list certain events as Old Style (OS). England finally faced up to the error and adjusted its calendar, 170 years after the Gregorian calendar's introduction in 1582.

As well, the enormous and most unusual ages apparently attained by numerous Biblical characters (see Genesis V) may well have been taken from inconsistent and occasional use of lunar cycles rather than solar. For instance, division by twelve makes some of these ages a lot more credible. Enoch is stated to have lived only 365 years (30+), and the age of his son, the legendary Methuselah, is given at 969 (80+) years.

It's a bit hard to assimilate it all, but as rendered by King James scholars, the pertinent verses of chapter V of Genesis read:

> 21 And Enoch lived sixty and five years, and begat Methuselah:
> 22 And Enoch walked with God after he begat Methuselah three hundred years, and begat sons and daughters:
> 23 And all the days of Enoch were three hundred sixty and five years:
> 24 And Enoch walked with God: and he *was* not; for God took him.
> 25 And Methuselah lived an hundred eighty and seven years, and begat Lamech:
> 26 And Methuselah lived after he begat Lamech seven hundred eighty and two years, and begat sons and daughters:
> 27 And all the days of Methuselah were nine hundred and sixty and nine years, and he died.
> 28 And Lamech lived an hundred eighty and two years, and begat a son:
> 29 And he called his name Noah, saying, This *same* shall comfort us concerning our work and toil of our hands, because of the ground which the LORD hath cursed.

Noah's Ark as pictured in 1846 by American Quaker artist, Edward Hicks (1780–1849). Some of God's later creatures were not in the lineup. *Philadelphia Museum of Art.*

30 And Lamech lived after he begat Noah five hundred ninety and five years, and begat sons and daughters:

31 And all the days of Lamech were seven hundred seventy and seven years: and he died.

32 And Noah was five hundred years old: and Noah begat Shem, Ham and Japheth.

One of the greater figures of astronomy was the German-born Sir Frederick William Herschel (1738–1822), the King's astronomer, who spotted an unknown planet in 1781 and tried to name it after his royal patron, King George III — an idea for Uranus that was rejected by the rest of the world. But Sir William was also interested in sunspots and determined that their presence had a very human impact. Herschel was never the Astronomer Royal, though he was a close worker with the fifth such worthy, Nevil Maskelyne (1732–1811), who held that office after 1765. Herschel was also assisted immensely by his younger sister, Caroline (1750–1848), who was a notable observer in her own right.

In 1801, based on the observations he made (at his home in Bath, and earlier records he located elsewhere), Herschel found that during periods when sunspots were scarce, the price of wheat in London was always higher. What impact the publication of this coincidence had on Parliamentary discussions relative to the enactment of Britain's infamous Corn Laws in 1815 has never been clear, and subsequent observations have not confirmed any kind of scientific correlation. Corn, in this context, did not refer exclusively to the maize grown mostly in North America but also referenced wheat and grains in general. These odious laws, revised in 1828 and repealed in their entirety in 1846, called for a tariff that kept the price of all foods in the British Isles higher than otherwise — which was just fine by the major landowners, many of whom sat in one of the Houses of Parliament but worked a severe disservice on the less well-to-do.

The Corn Laws were a direct underlying factor in the great distress that led to the emigration of many Irish in that period — to the great enrichment of North America, where most of them ended up. These laws had encouraged the mostly British landowners of Ireland to continue to ship their wheat across the Irish Sea to England, even while the natives were starving from the three-year-long potato blight.

Toward the end of the nineteenth century, another English astronomer got into the game when Sir Joseph Norman Lockyer (1836–1920), in analyzing the spectrum of the Sun, noted an unaccounted-for band near that of Sodium that he concluded was caused by the presence of a heretofore unknown element, which he called Helium (adapted from the classical Greek word for the Sun, *helios*). More than coincidentally, Lockyer was also the founder, editor, and publisher of the noteworthy and now international journal *Science.*

But Lockyer was not alone in this research; he had a notable collaborator in France — Pierre-Jules-César Janssen (1824–1907), who was lamed by a childhood accident. Janssen became so interested in the precise composition of solar emanations that he raised funds to establish a solar observatory near the crest of Mont Blanc, at 15,781 feet, the highest point in western Europe and above nearly half of Earth's atmosphere, with its blessedly effective filtering effect on harmful solar emanations. Not only did he cause the structure to be prefabricated — after the noted design engineer, Alexandre Gustave Eiffel, had given up on such a concept — but Janssen coincidentally arranged for full employment in Chamonix for the summers of 1892 and 1893 by hiring half the town's male population to carry the disassembled fifteen-ton structure up the mountain and then put it together. There were nearly 2,000 loads of material carried up the mountain (including the aging Janssen himself, who was taken up there three times). It was a week's work for one porter to deliver 150 pounds to the top of the mountain and come down again.

The Janssen Observatory when it was briefly in place near the summit of Mont Blanc. *Charles E. Matthews.*

Unfortunately, nothing great was learned by this exercise, despite its steep expense. The structure, resting as it did on snow, gradually slid downhill, tipped over, and with its instruments safely removed to a lower location on bedrock, was torn apart and removed by 1909. However, around the world, others were taking up the cause, and mountaintop observatories (mostly meteorological) became established, albeit temporarily, on high points in many countries.[5]

The Signal Service of the United States Army,[6] a branch of which morphed into the U.S. Weather Bureau and thence into the National Oceanic and Atmospheric Agency (NOAA) in 1970, had established year-round mountain stations in 1873: Pikes Peak in Colorado, Mount Washington in New Hampshire, and Point Barrow in Arkansas. Though federal budget cuts[7] soon forced the formal closing of the mountaintop facilities, the structure on 14,110-foot Pikes Peak was occupied until 1886 by a crew of astronomers led by the noteworthy director of Harvard Observatory, Edward Charles Pickering (1846–1919), still trying to ascertain what was really happening on the Sun.

During its period of occupation by the Signal Service, the operating staff did not live up to official expectations and thus did not effectively serve any useful meteorological purpose. This is demonstrated by the "discharge without character" in 1881 of Sgt. Timothy O'Keeffe for filling out the observation reports without (according to more than one whistleblower) "having made the requisite observations," which O'Keeffe had explained away with the words, "Washington doesn't know any better."[8]

Mount Washington was also abandoned by the Signal Service in 1887 (except for the summers, which were occupied for an additional five seasons). But this unique locality was reoccupied as a year-round weather recording station in 1932 by the late Joseph Brooks Dodge and his staff of four younger meteorologists, with much help from the Carriage Road owners and Colonel "Hen" Teague, then proprietor of Mount Washington's famed cog railway. This latter station — home of the highest human-recorded wind velocity — 231 miles per hour in April of 1934 — was somewhat of an offshoot from the site of much American meteorological research and discovery on Great Blue Hill, south of Boston. This site had been established in 1885 by Abbott Lawrence Rotch (1861–1912), a pioneer in modern meteorology and an equally philanthropic first cousin[9] to the mathematician-astronomer Percival Lowell.

Because of its unique geographical situation — there is no comparable height upwind for more than 5,000 miles — Mount Washington, though decidedly unexalted among the world's high points, boasts several glacial cirques around its flanks and remains the site of the strongest winds and most miserable weather regularly recorded by man. It is also an increasingly civilized facility, despite its enormously exposed situation; both television and FM radio transmitters (as well as a museum and its unique railroad terminus) have been located there too. However, southeast of the summit is the ravine (a former glacial cirque) named for the Rev. Edward Tuckerman (1817–1886), a pioneering lichenologist long associated with Amherst College, and although still popular with spring skiers (even though the site of an occasional related fatality), it was also the former site of a much visited, summertime tourist attraction in the form of its year-round snow arch. But no winter snow has lingered through the summer anywhere in the White Mountains since 1927,[10] coincidentally the year of the greatest autumnal floods heretofore recorded in New England history — an event that might well have been an unrecognized hurricane, moving northeastward parallel with the Gulf Stream.

In order to determine if there was water vapor in the thin atmosphere of Mars, V. M. Slipher established a temporary station at some 10,100 feet (on Schultz Peak in Flagstaff, Arizona) so as to be above a bit more of the Earth's atmosphere than Percival Lowell's observatory, which is situated at only 7,250 feet, an altitude that happens, quite coincidentally, to be very close to the three-quarter mark in the amount (and pressure) of Earth's atmosphere. However, William Wallace Campbell

(a)

(b)

Tuckerman Ravine Snow Arch (a and b) was a regular, late-season tourist attraction of the White Mountains, which lasted through the heat of every post-Pleistocene summer — shown here in 1869 — until the great autumnal storm (an unrecognized midseason hurricane?) of 1927. It hasn't been seen since. *Mount Washington Observatory.*

(1862–1938), then director of the Lick Observatory (being understandably skeptical of anything connected with the well-to-do amateur Lowell or his observatory) wangled the funds to set up a station on the summit of Mount Whitney, some 3,000 feet higher than Slipher's, only to find that, with even less of Earth's atmosphere to confuse the results, he had to admit to detecting some Martian water vapor too. But the Signal Service, Slipher, and Campbell were not looking for sunspots.

Somewhat more than parenthetically, it is worth noting that many of the early men of science in both Britain and America had taken Holy Orders at the start of their careers. Reverend Tuckerman's Ravine is drained by the Cutler River, which was named for the Reverend Manasseh Cutler (1742–1823) of Ipswich, a revolutionary war soldier and Massachusetts Congressman as well as an explorer of the New England mountains, an early member of the American Association of Arts and Sciences, and the founder of Ohio State University.

One of the more articulate modern students of sunspots was the late John Allen Eddy (1931–2009), the abstract of whose 1976 article in *Science* (Vol. 192, #4245, p. 1189) sums up the Maunder Minimum situation pretty much as it is presently known:

> It has long been thought that the Sun is a constant star of regular and repeatable behavior. Measurements of the radiative output, or solar constant, seem to justify the first assumption, and the record of periodicity in sunspot numbers is taken as evidence of the second. Both records, however, sample only the most recent history of the Sun.
>
> When we look at the longer record — of the last 1,000 years or so — we find indications that the Sun may have undergone significant changes in behavior, with possible terrestrial effects. Evidence for past solar change is largely of an indirect nature and should be subject to the most critical scrutiny. Most accessible and crucial to the basic issue of past constancy or inconstancy, is a long period in the late seventeenth and early eighteenth centuries when, some have claimed, almost no sunspots were seen. The period, from about 1645 until 1715, was pointed out in the 1890s by G. Spörer and E. W. Maunder, I have reexamined the contemporary reports and new evidence which has come to light since Maunder's time and conclude that the 70-year period was indeed a time when solar activity all but stopped. This behavior is wholly unlike the modern behavior of the Sun which we have come to accept as normal, and the consequences for solar and terrestrial physics seem to me profound.

*All truth is precious,*
*if not all divine*

— William Cowper (1731–1800)
Hope Book 1

Machu Picchu in Peru

# VI
# Various Diaries

*Diary, n. A daily record of that part of one's life, which he can relate to himself without blushing.*

— A. Bierce, *The Devil's Dictionary* (1911)

One of the earliest diarists whose work achieved widespread (though unintended) popularity was Samuel Pepys (1633–1703), second secretary of the Royal Navy, whose private comments during the decade of the 1650s on life in Stuart-ruled Great Britain gave substance to the later contention of Charles Dickens that the rule of the Stuarts was "an unmitigated disaster" for England. Nevertheless, Pepys's diary, disregarding its occasional libidinous passages, with its tidbits on the Admiralty's fruitless obsession with finding the fabled Northwest Passage and its discussion of the Second Dutch War of 1654, the Great Plague of 1655, and London's Great Fire of 1656, is helpful in learning some of the thinking that went on in the ruling circles of England. Unfortunately, it touches only minimally on scientific matters. Therefore, we shall proceed to look at other forms of diaries.

A founding member of The American Alpine Club, then a scientific organization much concerned with orogeny and the study of glaciers, was the long-lived astronomer and founder of the science of dendrochronology, Andrew Ellicott Douglass (1867–1962). When he was employed in the years 1895–1901 by the mathematician and philanthropist Percival Lowell (a grandson of the John Amory Lowell who introduced Jean-Louis Agassiz to America) he began to search for additional means (following the dictum advanced by Ignaz Venetz) of dating any significant variations in solar performance that may have taken place before

Galileo began pointing his theological controversy-causing instrument at the Sun. Lowell had established his observatory in 1894 on a low mesa west of Flagstaff, Arizona, at 7,250 feet above sea level in the midst of a widespread ponderosa pine forest that was supported in the 1890s, according to Douglass, by an annual precipitation of twenty-four inches. However, by one century later, it was barely averaging three-fourths of that amount — and some years, far less.

All interested scholars already knew — from hints between the lines of ancient manuscripts — that during the time since man began keeping written records, such meteorological variations as may have occurred had not been widely catastrophic (except as specified during Noah's event). But the details of tree-ring analysis still might offer a shorter-range clue as to past climates and perhaps a hint as to what might be expected in the future. What Douglass (and his successors in the science he begat) learned opened up a new vista on the determination of Earth's historical record for several thousand years further into the past — in many respects matched and reinforced by the work of Dr. Antevs, discussed on the next page.

Annual rings — a feature of all trees growing in temperate zones where there is an active seasonal growing period — can be close or wide, depending on numerous factors. These can include the fertility of the soil, exposure to the Sun, consistency and type of precipitation, air quality, insect infestations, forest fires, and any other factors that might impinge on the growing conditions in the neighborhood of the tree. Because we can easily note these factors operating in the present, scientists logically assume that all growing things in the same area are (or have been) equally and collectively affected by similar, if not identical, factors in the past. A quarter-inch diameter core extracted from a youthful tree can therefore be compared with part of a similar core taken from an older, perhaps even dead, tree in the same forest or at least physically close enough to have experienced some of the same overall growing conditions.

The process continues by finding patterns of comparable rings in trees of varying ages and is thus able to be extended serially from younger trees (whose age can be matched to a current calendar) to increasingly older trees and thence into the wooden beams of old houses, ancient cliff dwellings, churches, temples, and castles (even to logs found in old avalanche debris or moraines). They can thereby provide an accurate means of reaffirming folklore and legend or dating years of catastrophe or construction, as well as — our concern here — giving reliable information about the nearby growing conditions (climate) of times past. This procedure has been enhanced by the more modern use of $carbon_{14}$ and $beryllium_{10}$ half-life dating systems.

Andrew Ellicott Douglass was the locator of Percival Lowell's Observatory but argued with his employer over the *"canali"* of Mars and was terminated. In Tucson, he later achieved great fame for his development of the science of dendrochronology through the study of tree-ring counts. *Lowell Observatory Archives.*

Tree-ring counting among the Bristlecone Pines of the Sierra Nevada Range has determined that these particular trees are very long-lived, indeed. One such tree, intemperately cut in 1964, is said to have yielded 4,844 rings, predating even the legendary Pharonic pyramids of Giza.

• • •

The Swedish-born scientist Ernst Valdemar Antevs (1888–1974) was a student under the equally Swedish Baron Gerard De Geer (1855–1943), the geologist who pioneered the study of Quaternary phenomena. He was also a companion in research with Kirk Bryan (more to follow) and associated in his later years with the University of Arizona. Coming to America in 1920, Antevs initially made his name through the study of varves (annual layers of clay, deposited in pro-glacial lakes). Once established in the New World, he started at the bottom of a wall in a disused clay pit on the southerly side of Long Island, and — after preparing it carefully — photographed a tall column of its very obvious layers. He then carried a picture of that columnar pattern northward to other clay pits, comparing various distinctive annual patterns of varve thicknesses from the upper layers of one disused clay pit to those at a lower level in another (sufficiently nearby) during the period of glacial wastage that experienced the same basic local weather. Then he was able to carry a distinctive pattern across Long Island Sound to the mainland of Connecticut and thence ever farther north (although he encountered a potential discontinuity near the latitude of Claremont, NH) as far as Lake Timiskaming, near Hudson's Bay. In so doing, he evolved a chronology of some 11,000 years, for varves, very much like tree rings, form in regular thickness patterns depending on the local weather conditions. The lighter-colored, somewhat sandier segment of each varve is deposited when the lake surface is disturbed by waves, as much more water is in transit during the summers, then grades into the darker (finer) segment — the components of which settle out only when the lake surface starts to freeze over and the meltwater input becomes less during the fall and winter. It ends with a crisper cutoff marking the often suddenness of the spring breakup.

Varved clays, like tree rings, can be read to tell of past climate, such as warm, active summers and those of shorter duration when the weather might have been

Ernst Antevs carefully measured the varves (annual layers of fine mineral silt) accumulated in New England lakes (now clay pits) and — coupled with experience from his native Sweden — was the first to put a close-to-actual date on the final melting away of the last phase of Pleistocene continental glaciers. *University of Arizona.*

a bit cooler. In many ways, the study of tree rings, other paleobotanical remnants, and varved clays can also be compared to the work of Bishop Ussher and others in calculating the climate as well as precise years, as was done by the Biblical chronologies of who begat whom in what year of their lives, and so forth.

• • •

Another interesting diary of Northern Hemisphere climate — but only for the last millennium — is the record of when the arctic ice pack could be seen from the hills of Iceland. This record (see table) shows a trend from the time of first settlement in 881 CE, which was warmer than at present, and then grades into a significantly cooler period, closely coinciding with the Maunder Minimum and Little Ice Age in Europe:

| Period | Number of Weeks Observed | Sun Spot Activity |
|---|---|---|
| 881–1010 | 0 – 4 | |
| 1011–1211 | 0 – 5 | |
| 1212–1387 | 6 – 9 | Spörrer Minimum |
| 1388–1586 | 2 – 3 | |
| 1587–1798 | 6 –22 | Maunder Minimum |
| 1799–1879 | 7 – 40 | |
| 1889–1964 | 9 – 13 | |

There are some otherwise ascertainable and more precise dates mixed in with this Icelandic data that emphasize the onset of the impending cooling trend discussed just below. In 1126, near the end of the prior warm period, the Holy See in Rome had established a bishopric[1] in Greenland to oversee the two dozen parishes that had arisen there in the decades after Leif Ericsson and his father (a Norseman of a different color) had found a "green" land to the west of Iceland. With the apparent acceptance of the skraelings[2] (native Amerindians), this bishopric grew to include such additional religious amenities as an Augustinian monastery and a Benedictine convent, valiantly striving to sustain a European lifestyle in the more brutal Arctic region that is unsupported by the warmth of the Gulf Stream. (The Augustinians, or Austins, also operated shelters at the crests of several alpine passes, most notably the Great Saint Bernard and the Moncenisio. Saint Scholastica [d. 542], sister of Saint Benedict, was the first to develop educational facilities for young females. But on September 20, 1448, Pope Nicholas V [Tomasso Parentucelli] reported there had apparently been some change of attitude by the skraelings with reference to "the island of Greenland, situated at the uttermost end of the earth.")

> The island, belonging to the Kingdom of Norway, and under the ecclesiastical jurisdiction of the Archbishop of Trondheim, received the faith of Christ almost six [actually nearer four] centuries ago, through the piety of blessed King Olaf [Saint Olaf II (Haraldsson) regnant from 1015 to 1028] and preserved it steadfastly and inviolably in accordance with the tradition of the Roman Church, and the Apostolic See. After their conversion, the people of this island, with untiring and characteristic devotion, erected many temples to the worship of God and his saints, as well as a magnificent cathedral,[3] in which divine worship was diligently celebrated, until about thirty years ago, when God permitting it, a barbarous and pagan fleet from neighboring shores invaded the island, laying waste to the land with fire and sword . . . . Just nine parish churches were left standing.

In different records, we learn that in 1425, nearly three centuries after its founding, the shepherd of the cathedral of St. Nicholas at Gardar sent his final report to Rome. Thereafter, silence! This sad event was mentioned in a letter by the Spanish-born cardinal Roderic Llancoli de Borja (1431–1503), later Pope Alexander VI in 1492, the same year that — regardless of any possible feelings on the part of the Abenakis, Aleuts, Arapahoes, Assiniboines, Aztecs, Blackfeet, Cherokees, Chippewa, Cree, Dakotas, Eries, Incas, Innuits, Kootenai, Lakotas, Mohawks, Navajos, Pequods, Seminoles, Skraelings, Tlingits, Uncpapas, Utes, Wampanoags, Zunis, and others — he divided ownership of the New World along the line of 46°37′ west longitude,[4] for the "benefit" of the Spanish crown (his people) and to the presumed detriment of the Portuguese. Then he issued a papal bulla, stating:

> It has been reported to us that in the Diocese of Gardar in Greenland, situated at the confines of the known world, the inhabitants, because of the scarcity of bread, wine and oil, live for the most part on dried fish and milk products. Wherefore because of the difficulty of passing through such immense quantities of ice, and likewise because of the poverty of the land, and the scant means of living, ships rarely visit its shores. We have learned that no vessel has touched there during the past eighty years, and if a voyage be made at all, it must be in the month of August, when the ice has broken up. On this account, during eighty years no bishop or priest has resided personally among those people, and by reason of this, we are informed that many who were formerly

The ruins of the Norse Cathedral at Gardar, a modern adventure tourism goal. *From a travel brochure.*

> Catholics have forgotten the faith of their baptism, and that no memory of the Christian religion is found, except a corporal [linen], which is shown to the people once a year, and on which it is said the last priest who officiated there consecrated the body of Christ a hundred years ago. In consideration of these things, Innocent VIII, our predecessor of happy memory, wishing to provide a proper pastor for these forlorn people, conferred with his brethren, of whom we were one, and elected Matthias, our venerable brother, a member of the Order of St. Benedict, a professed monk, at our suggestion, and while we were in minor orders, to be Bishop of Garder.

In those early days of the Great Reformation, the new pope still unrealistically but optimistically thought his words would carry weight in far-off lands that had lately become seriously out of communion with Rome. He mandated that everyone take good care of Matthias en route to Greenland on his new assignment: "To him everything must be free, other things to the contrary notwithstanding." But there is no record that he ever got there!

In fact, the five-century-old Norse colonization of Greenland was doomed from the start by the persistence of the settlers (read as "invaders") from Norway in applying traditional European and Christian methodology in an environment where these milder-climate agricultural and subsistence policies could not be sustained. Despite the continuance of Gulf Stream warmth to reach high latitudes in Scandinavia, the onset of the Little Ice Age simply made the colony's survival a bit more unlikely. Though in the end, it was the hatred they engendered among the Innuits (skraelings) that brought on the finishing blow to the colony's survival.

Then, in 1657, as a further part of various Scandinavian misunderstandings, the Danes unwisely declared war on Sweden, whose kingdom was simultaneously deeply involved in a war with Russia, and gifted with some of the best strategic brains in contemporary Europe.[5] This event brought into prominence the Swedish general Carl Gustav Wrangel (1613–1676) and the military engineer Erik Jönnsson Dahlbergh (1625–1703), who was later in the service of King Charles II of England, both of whom, under the overall leadership of King Carl Gustav X (1622–1660), set out to teach the Danes a lesson. Despite the approach of winter, the Swedish army marched quickly west from its venture in Poland, retaking Schwerin and Bremen en route and overwhelming the Jutland peninsula, much to the shock of the Danes, who controlled the sea (where it was liquid). King Gustav's forces then laid siege to Copenhagen, on Zeeland, by marching all his forces (complete with artillery and cavalry) across the frozen water adjacent to the Kattegat in the ten days between January 30 and February 8, 1658.[6] This unexpected maneuver not only cost the Danes dearly but also highlights the fact that the European midwinter (in the period of the Maunder Minimum and the Little Ice Age) was sufficiently cold that the normally "punky" sea ice was sturdy enough to support the weight of all this military materiel and man, as well as horse, power. The ensuing Peace of Copenhagen (in 1660) resulted in Danish loss of sovereignty over most of southern Sweden, and largely set into place the current boundaries of all Scandinavia. The French diplomat Hughes de Terlon, who was traveling with the Swedish army, reported to King Louis XIV as follows:

> I assure Your Majesty that it was so cold that one had to use an axe to cut up the bread as well as break up beer and wine barrels. The pieces were then allowed to thaw whereupon they hardly had any taste left. Meat was put into heated pans but it was mostly inedible. The King of Sweden merely laughed at such discomforts although he shared them. His only thought was to succeed in his daring plan.

• • •

The most potent of the tools that modern man has found to help in dating the past with real credibility is the more recently evolved technique of radiocarbon dating. This began as a project by researchers at the University of Chicago on the suggestion of the outstanding, Italian-born, Nobel Prize Laureate (1938) physicist Enrico Fermi (1901–1954). It was completed under the leadership of Willard Frank Libby (1908–1980), another one-time team member of the Manhattan Project, for which he received the Nobel Prize in Chemistry in 1960. He offered a homey example of the process in his acceptance address as follows:

> We are [all] in the radiocarbon-dating business as soon as this has been said, for it is clear from the set of assumptions that have been given that organic matter, while it is alive, is in equilibrium with the cosmic radiation: that is, all the radiocarbon atoms which disintegrate in our bodies are replaced by the Carbon-14 contained in the food we eat, so that while we are alive we are part of a great pool which contains the cosmic-ray produced radiocarbon. The specific activity is maintained at the level of about fourteen disintegrations per minute per gram by the mixing action of the biosphere and hydrosphere. We assimilate cosmic-ray produced Carbon-14 atoms at just the rate that the Carbon-14 atoms in our bodies disappear to form Nitrogen-14. At the time of death, however, the assimilation process stops abruptly. There is no longer any process by which the Carbon-14 from the atmosphere can enter our bodies. Therefore, at the time of death the radioactive disintegration process takes over in an uncompensated manner and, according to the law of radio-active decay, after 5,600 years the carbon that was in our bodies while we were alive will show half the specific Carbon-14 radioactivity that it shows now. Since we have evidence that this has been true for tens of thousands of years, we should expect to find that a body 5,600 years old would be one-half as radioactive as a present-day living organism. This appears to be true. Measurements of old artifacts of historically known age have shown this to be so within the experimental errors of measurement.

Libby's seventeen-page typescript lecture to the Nobel Committee, written on December 12 of that year, contains other fascinating tidbits of the program he headed — including references to verifying his dating system against Egyptian mummies of a precisely known date, analysis of redwood timber from a tree stump with a ring count of 2,908 years, and an amusing reference to the need

to obtain modern methane for comparison with that from a deep oil well (the municipal sewage treatment facility of Baltimore provided an appropriate sample). It concludes as follows:

> The large number of people who have contributed to the development of the radiocarbon dating technique, several of whom I have mentioned today, but many of whom I have been unable to mention, are largely responsible for whatever success it has had. We now have several thousand radiocarbon dates throughout the fields of archeology, geology, meteorology, oceanography, and other areas. From the examination of the results, it is possible to form an opinion as to the general reliability and general weaknesses of the method. I am sure that Dr. Arnold[7] would agree with me in saying that it has lived up to our fondest hopes. It was clear from the beginning that there would be difficulties about the samples. Anyone knows it is possible to get dirt into solid matter which is lying on the ground, even if it is there only for a brief period, let alone thousands or tens of thousands of years. The saving aspect of the situation, however, is that it is very much more difficult to mix molecules in such a way that they cannot be separated chemically, particularly in the case of substances such as charcoal and wood and cloth, and even in certain cases for limestone and shale. One can separate and distinguish the contaminant from the original material and in this way disclose the real radiocarbon content. The researches of a number of people have validated the assumption that it is possible and that, indeed, it is not too difficult to obtain authentic samples in the field. In general samples may have to be inspected with some care under a relatively high-powered glass and then be treated with properly chosen chemicals. But all of these things can be done and with techniques that are no more difficult than those used by the average hospital technician, and a sample can be obtained which should give authentic radiocarbon dates. The dating technique itself is one which requires care, but which can be carried out by adequately trained personnel who are sufficiently serious-minded about it. It is something like the discipline of surgery — cleanliness, care, seriousness, and practice. With these things it is possible to obtain radiocarbon dates which are consistent and which may help roll back the pages of history and reveal to mankind something more about his ancestors, and in this way perhaps about his future.

• • •

It has, so far, been impossible to determine how long these minute electronic (cosmic ray) items have been bombarding Earth from space, possibly ever since time began. Nor is anyone all that sure where they come from — perhaps left-over particles from Monsignor Lemaître's big bang or perhaps ionic bits from events like the Crab Nebula explosion of one millennium ago. They come from all directions, not just from within the solar system; they appear to be a factor in the aging process that affects all living matter — and are involved in the break-down of other ionic items that also bombard Earth from "out there," including those wonderful little dating mechanisms, carbon$_{14}$ and beryllium$_{10}$, that have been so helpful in recent times to scientists trying to determine the dating of events in Earth's past.

One of the most erudite of those scientists was the late Jack Eddy, from whose works on solar behavior we have learned much and continue to lean on heavily. With regard to what has happened to Earth's atmosphere under the influence of modern man, in a NASA publication,[8] Eddy offered a doggerel takeoff from Stevenson's *A Child's Garden of Verses and Underwoods* (1913):

The rain is raining all around,
It falls on field and tree.
"Big drops of $H_2SO_4$"
"And chunks of 10-Be."

Unfortunately for the carbon$_{14}$ dating system (not beryllium$_{10}$), it starts to become seriously unreliable for the dating of vegetative matter that began life after 1900. By that time, the man-induced insertion of carbon dioxide into the atmosphere, and thence into all living vegetation, had so overwhelmed the more subtle carbon$_{14}$ particles in the atmosphere that this dating mechanism cannot be used with confidence on such material.

This regrettable result has come about because modern man has taken to using the atmosphere as a societal dump. The increasingly obvious result is far worse than the "traditional" acid rain that began doing terrible things in the 1920s to the softwood forests of eastern North America as a result of the burning of Mid-western soft coal. Due to the worldwide spread of this polluting process, man is now dumping into the atmosphere increasing tons of chemicals that nature never intended and that the atmosphere simply cannot cope with or eliminate, so the ugly stuff just accumulates in the air we all breathe, thereby affecting all life on the planet. If, as many religious leaders insist, man was intended by God to subdue and control every other creature on Earth, then we have recently commenced to do a very irresponsible job of it. It is one thing to accumulate a mess in one's own backyard, but no society has ever approved of dumping one's mess into everyone else's — the only air that everyone has to breathe.

• • •

Meteorological experts place much value in accuracy and consistency of observations that may occasionally appear unnecessary to some collectors (such as Sergeant O'Keeffe) but have long-term value in climatology. Therefore, the U.S. Signal Service commander, General William Babcock Hazen (1830–1887), mandated early on that whenever any weather observation facility was planned to be moved — however slightly — simultaneous observations would be maintained from both the old and the new positions for at least one year so that any local irregularities could be recorded and later accounted for. Thus, it is that meteorological people are very loath to relocate their instruments once a local recording system has been started.

Continuous weather records were initially kept at various locations in Europe, starting with Berlin in 1700. Though not the first (Philadelphia in 1738), the oldest continuous official weather statistics kept in North America were those of the station founded at New Haven, Connecticut, where reliable temperature records began in 1780 and precipitation records in 1804.

Taken in twelve-year increments (to span a complete sunspot cycle) those from 1804 through 1815 show an average Fahrenheit temperature of 49.33° and average annual precipitation of 46.1 inches. Those in the final cycle (1959–1970[9]) show that the average temperature had risen a full Fahrenheit degree, to 50.33° while the precipitation had dropped by 9 inches (22.9 centimeters) to 37.1 inches.

Since the time of Playfair and Agassiz, mankind has learned ever more facts of Earth history, as recounted by students of past climates using the methods described above. We have learned that — within the past million or so years — there have been four major episodes of widespread glaciation (that is, not merely in the mountains), the last of which may not yet be concluded, for the politically charged outcry relative to "acid rain" and current global warming may be man's unintentional, but most seriously hurtful, contributions of impact to the numerous cycles of varying length that have affected Earth's climate.

• • •

The biggest centers of continental glaciation in the Pleistocene were in the areas of Hudson's Bay and the Baltic Sea, though glacial ice appears to have spread around much of Western Europe from one core location in the Alps, another in Britain, and a third but lesser one in North America from a core location on Vancouver Island.[10] The immense weight of the major masses of ice, believed to be nearly five miles thick at their centers and maxima, is credited with depressing the crustal layers of Earth so as to produce these two modern, but quite shallow, arms of the ocean. The frequent (once or twice in a human lifetime) minor earthquakes that affect eastern North America are interpreted as a sign of ongoing "isostatic rebound" due to the release of all that weight of ice.[11] Furthermore, it appears from studies of ancient American middens, bone fragments, and other excavations that the aboriginal human inhabitants of North America were accompanied by mammoths,[12] horses, and other (presumably edible) critters that also came eastward from Asia by way of the land bridge that existed during those periods of lowered sea level when up to 200 feet of ocean water became glacial ice on land.

In addition, paleontologists, working in the prehistoric middens (also known as town dumps) of North America aided by scientists of other disciplines have noted there were no less than three major waves of invasion by way of this now and again (Diomede) land bridge (consider it an ancient isthmus). Each such invasion caused the descendants of the previous migrations to be pushed a bit farther east or south.[13]

A landmark of late Ice Age precipitation, the popular "benches" of present-day Salt Lake City form part of a historic park and mark the shoreline for hundreds of miles around the periphery of the Pleistocene era's glacial Lake Bonneville. *W. L. Putnam III.*

In the Pleistocene era, the record shows there were also land bridges, due to lowered sea level, that occasionally connected Australia with southeast Asia,[14] during the early (but not later) Pleistocene era, thereby allowing the independent development of several species we now see as unique and native to that large, semi-isolated landmass — the emu, platypus, kangaroo, koala, and even a separate branch of *Homo sapiens* (complete with the didgeridoo).

During those frigid episodes, there were also substantial glaciers throughout the Rocky Mountains of Colorado, Wyoming, and Utah — the westmost of which furnished a meltwater output sufficient to support a large Glacial Lake Bonneville that (when full) drained northward into the Snake River.[15] Today, it is visible as the much reduced and very brackish Great Salt Lake. The high-rent residential district of modern Salt Lake City is up on "the benches," which can be traced horizontally for miles and represent the sandy beaches marking the overflow level of this Lake Bonneville.

These continental and expanded mountain glaciers, which gained all their frozen water from the ocean, were akin to what presently remains in Greenland and Antarctica and behaved the same way as the mountain glaciers described by Professor Forbes in chapter III. They pushed outward and covered the land in front, or below, with slowly moving ice, shoving everything ahead of their fronts in the form of terminal moraines and gravelly outwash. "Shoving" may not be the best word, overall, for a glacier's motion, for ice melts under pressure and thus eases its way around some obstacles. Glaciers flow, as well as push, rip, scrape, and carry. (Anyone who wants to see the full glacial process in action can take a few weeks to visit the Malaspina Glacier of coastal Alaska, where trees have even taken root on the morainal fringe of this glacier where it has expanded out of the Saint Elias Range into the Pacific Ocean.) Traveling northwestward by boat from the port of Yakutat in Alaska across the broad mouth of Disenchantment Bay to near the edge of the Malaspina (named for Alessandro Malaspina [1754–1810], an Italian navigator under royal commission from Spain who charted the West Coast of North America in 1791), one is struck by the fact that many of the evergreen trees on the vegetation-covered fringe of this piedmont glacier have been tipped from the normal vertical status of a growing tree — as deeply buried ice finally melts, or other parts move forward — and then resumed normal growth, trying to grow vertically once again.

The smaller sized material once carried by a glacier, and sometimes overrun by the ice or dropped in place where the glacier has run out of sufficiently cold weather, is known by various names besides that derived from the French "moraine." The English call it "boulder clay," a term that is very descriptive of its

Twenty feet (6 meters) in any dimension and perched on a skyline ridge at 3,721 feet above sea level, the Glen Boulder also catches the eye southwest from Highway 16 through Pinkham Notch, New Hampshire. *Mount Washington Observatory.*

content. Yankee farmers call it "hard pan," a term that describes well its innate resistance to pick and shovel.

This process of glaciation has not occurred without leaving a few spectacular remnants. When a mile of ice covered even the 6,288.1 foot[16] summit of Mount Washington, its motion ripped a huge hunk of rock from its bedrock birthplace near the summit. When times got warmer, it was gently lowered onto a ridge crest several miles to the south-by-southeast, where the Glen Boulder resides securely and spectacularly to this day, near the timberline, some 3,729 feet above the ocean, 2,000 feet above the adjacent valley, and more than 2,500 feet below the crest of the Old Rockpile, as this mountain is affectionately known to the scientists who inhabit its crest.

In support of his often repeated contention that the ice periods of the Pleistocene era were "worldwide and synchronous," Kirk Bryan[17] would cite, among other things, the analyses he had made with Claude Carroll Albritton Jr. (reported in the August 1943 *American Journal of Science*, p. 470ff). In studying the soils of the mountainous area of West Texas where the two men had grown up (near sites where fossil mammoth bones have also been found), they summarized their findings:

> A complex soil near Praesum in the Davis Mountains seems to satisfy the requirements for providing a large amount of paleoclimatological data. According to one interpretation, this soil records three stages of relative aridity, during which caliche was deposited in the subsoil, and two intervening stages of moister climate, during which the previously deposited caliche[18] was partially or entirely dissolved. This interpretation is in harmony with the climatic evidence in the adjacent valley flats, which are underlain by three bodies of alluvium separated by partial disconformities. On the evidence of the alluvium itself, it had already been postulated that deposition took place during relatively humid times, whereas erosion of the valley flats in gullies now identifiable on the surfaces preserved along disconformities, occurred during relatively arid times. The pedologic and geologic records seem therefore to be in harmony with each other.

Bryan had also telegraphed the import of his study with a paper in the edition of *Science* dated October 16, 1925 (p. 338), in which he noted that past episodes of arroyo cutting had been severe and were of various ages, including up to historical times. He noted that the most prominent erosional features seemed to have developed mostly within the prior century:

> It is not, however, the purpose of this paper to discuss the origin of the arroyos but to put in compact and usable form the existing information as to the dates when these processes have been recorded in only a few instances, and the more or less hazy recollections of early settlers are the only source of information regarding some streams. In the accounts of travelers, in the notes of early land surveys and in other local records there are many valuable historical data that as yet are largely unused in a systematic way. With the passage of years such information becomes more difficult to obtain, and it is hoped that the notes presented herewith will stimulate the gathering of more complete data on the time of stream trenching in the arid southwest.

VII

# The Astronomers

*He stretcheth out the north over the empty place, and hangeth the earth upon nothing.*
— Job 26:7 (KJB)

The English word "science" comes to us from the Latin *scientia*, which means "knowledge." And of all the various sciences that are found in a modern lexicon, by far the purest is that of astronomy. That word by itself is a bit of a misnomer, for it is derived from the words *astra* (Latin for stars) and *nomos* (Greek for name); whereas *logos* is the Greek word for "study." The medieval astrologers, who knew a lot of star names, mostly derived from the nomadic Arabs, did their thing by studying how and where various heavenly bodies lined up, and in so doing, preempted the more appropriate term. But these folk were only interested in foretelling events according to how, when, and where certain stars (mostly the planets) appeared in the sky, and they did not care much what was actually going on with these distant points of light. The modern scientists who do their thing by looking through increasingly sophisticated telescopes are only occasionally concerned with naming what they see; rather, they are very seriously concerned with the detailed study of what they see and how it might relate to humanity and the planet we all live on.

In an extension of this process — and also by asking himself and his professional staff, "How did it all get started?" — Percival Lowell, in 1902, ordered his new and surprisingly talented assistant, Vesto Melvin Slipher, to look into the spectrum (so as to determine its composition) of a faint spiral nebula, Andromeda, which Lowell and others thought might be another solar system in the process of formation. It turned out, however, on Slipher's pioneering and thorough

The Discovery Channel Telescope at Lowell Observatory is one of the largest, most versatile, and modern instruments in the world. *Lowell Observatory.*

inspection, to be but one of quite a number of other galaxies far outside the Milky Way, most of which he deduced by spectrum analysis — the astronomically famous "red shift" — to be moving away from Earth at astounding speeds.

Regardless of this historic trivia or the earlier esoteric wordplay, astronomy is the purest of all sciences because no scientist has ever put his hand on a star or visited a distant galaxy. Everything that has ever been learned about such things by these folk has been done by simple, Berra-type observation, followed by extensive laboratory, or reasoned, analysis of what has been seen, along with a great deal of very high-class mathematical deduction. As an elementary instance, the average distance of 93,000,000 miles to the Sun, Earth's parent star, has been determined by the arithmetic process everyone is supposed to learn in the eighth grade — trigonometry. During the course of making this determination, however, astronomers found that Earth's orbit around the Sun was not circular but slightly elliptical; we are presently about 2 percent closer to our parent star during the Northern Hemisphere winter. But this will change, as it has in the past, due to an ongoing process known as the precession of the equinoxes. As well, the declination of Earth's rotational axis from the plane of its orbit also varies from its present 23.5° (which appears to be near the end part of its range). But this too has changed regularly in the past with consequent variations in the habitability of various regions of Earth[1] as well as producing the seasonal variations that are important to almost all life on our home planet.

The most basic of these orbital facts have been known to (naked eye) observers of the heavens for a great many years. In 129 BCE, the brilliant but short-lived Greek astronomer Hipparchos was the first to measure, again by precise trigonometry, the distance of the Moon from Earth. He also compiled a star catalog, but in so doing, made reference to similar such efforts by Babylonian stargazers three millennia earlier. Continuing that regional tradition, most of the unelected rulers of subsequent Islamic countries — aghas, beys, caliphs, or deys — employed court astronomers to read the heavens and offer advice. Hipparchos observed that the positions of stars — in his day — were measurably different, but in a consistent and logical manner, from the locations assigned by his learned Babylonian predecessors. This precession turns out to be a major alteration, sort of a slow-motion wobble, and was subsequently determined to have a period taking 25,772 earthly revolutions around the Sun.

The North Pole of Earth's axis is currently pointed to within a very few degrees of the star astronomers call Polaris, the North Star. However, the direction (alignment) of the axis is not rigidly fixed in space. Due mostly to the combined gravitational influences of the Sun and the Moon, the axis wobbles, somewhat like a waning top, in a circle. The radius of the wobble is the size of the obliquity of that axis to the plane of Earth's orbit. It takes 25,772 years to make one full such wobble around the circle of Earth's orbit. In 12,886 years, the wobble will be half completed, and at that time the Northern Hemisphere summer will occur in the part of Earth's orbit that winter now occurs and vice versa. Our current summer constellations will be the ones we see in winter and vice versa. Rather than thinking of it as an unsettling wobble of the Earth's axis, one can think of it as a slow (in human life span terms) change of the seasons, the equinoxes, or the solstices. It was this very slow change in the apparent alignment of many stars that was first noted by Hipparchos when he found that his Babylonian predecessors' star positions were not as he saw things in his day.

That matter took several thousand years to be noticed, but the much shorter individual human life span issue affects the judgment of humanity in many additional ways. Because our lives are so relatively short compared to that of the planet we live on, we tend to see as catastrophic a great number of events that are routine in a geologic sense. The litany of such actions is substantial, but our newspapers and history books report geologically commonplace events as disasters, such as landslides of steep terrain, rivers washing away (or creating) mid-stream islands, storms taking away (or bringing back) beaches, volcanoes pouring lava into oceans and ash into the skies, and earthquakes sliding apparently great slices of the earth up, down, and sideways. These things — even intense human disasters like the fatal collapse of Alberta's Turtle Mountain on the night of April 29, 1903, or more recent tsunamis — have been happening for at least four billion years and are all normal processes in the ongoing transformation of the surface of our planet.

• • •

Milutin Milankovitch (1879–1958) was not an astronomer by training. He was a multitalented construction engineer of Serbian nationality. However, he had the misfortune to be imprisoned shortly after the outbreak of the Great War[2] (1914–1918) when the Austrian overlords of his nation interrupted his honeymoon with the accusation that he was an enemy alien. So while his young wife called on all her influential relatives to see if, or how, she could wangle his freedom, he languished in jail — thinking (presumably among other things) about the various cycles within the major fact of Earth's "regular" motion around the Sun.

In due course, Milankovitch got to pondering the cause of ice ages and climate change, trying in particular to determine what sort of force, or system, had caused the origin of the extensive coal deposits that had been discovered by Austrian explorers on the presently barren and frigid Arctic island of Spitsbergen 500 kilometers north of the tip end of Norway. No visibly operative force of nature could account for their derivation since it was obvious there had to have been a semitropical environment on Spitsbergen for all that one-time vegetation to have accumulated.

Milutin Milankovitch was a little-known Serbian scientist who left a major mark on the study of Earth history by virtue of his intense and detailed arithmetic application of astronomical facts. *Lowell Observatory Archives.*

By the time his wife had obtained his release, Milankovitch was ready to put his thoughts into form, and fortunately, he was also able to become attached to the Hungarian Academy of Sciences at Budapest, where he spent the remaining war years, until the complete collapse of Austria-Hungary in October of 1918. By that time, Milankovitch's published calculations had earned him a place in numerous scientific discussions, including some with Alfred Wegener. He began to formulate a mathematical mechanism to account for that massive coal formation[3] near the North Pole that involved the shifting of the surface layers of the earth relative to the poles and the equator. Unfortunately, while he acquired a useful collaborator in Julius von Hann (1839–1921), a distinguished Austrian meteorologist, with the premature death of Wegener in 1930, he lost a more valued collaborator relative to continental drift. However, his astronomic calculations continued.

The resulting Milankovitch Cycles, where certain variables combine to seriously affect Earth's climate, are based on three factors: (1) the eccentricity of Earth's orbit around the Sun, (2) the axial tilt of Earth's poles of rotation relative to the plane of that orbit, and (3) the precession of the equinoxes. These mechanical variables are also influenced by gravitational attractions from other heavenly bodies in the solar system according to the following order of importance: the Moon,[4] the Sun, Jupiter, and Saturn. When certain factors combined in these various cycles, he deduced the cause of massive changes in terrestrial climate. Note that it doesn't take a great deal of temperature change to cause precipitation to occur as either rain or snow. Water is commonplace on Earth in all three forms — vapor, liquid, and solid.

In the years after the Great War, and with increasing vigor after its sequel 1939–1945, reinforcements for the Serbian mathematician's ideas were provided by fellow geologists and, interestingly, more than a few oceanographers. Research petrologists were able to determine that the magnetic orientation of certain minerals in crystalline igneous formations pointed to different magnetic pole locations than at present. They were also able to determine that within certain sedimentary formations of Permian Age, exposed in New England and elsewhere, were remnants of glacial moraines — including, of all things, a varved clay (now hardened into slate) formation almost under Harvard Yard! Even more astounding was the discovery, from ever more sophisticated petrological analysis, that there had been glaciation on a global scale as far back as the Cambrian era. In the end, ice ages turned out to have been a significant (perhaps regular) part of Earth's history, not merely in the last million years, but half a billion and a billion years earlier.

• • •

In the mid-twentieth century, oceanographers — many of whom were based out of the once sleepy vacation port of Woods Hole, Massachusetts — took to probing and searching analysis of sediments found in cores taken from the deeper ocean beds. While they started nearby in the more accessible North Atlantic Ocean, they soon became more curious. In due course, scientists of the Woods Hole Oceanographic Institute were able to deduce what sank to the ocean floor and when, for a period covering thousands of years, by examining the melting of the icebergs derived from the mountain glaciers of Greenland that drifted south in the spring of each year. They not only came across various parts of the Royal Mail Ship the *Titanic*, but they learned (by careful study of the accumulation of these iceberg droppings) how the pattern of southward drift had changed over the millennia. From this finding, it was but another small step to go farther afield to the Indian Ocean, where the oceanographers knew they could find a less cluttered record of what else had sunk under the waves and slowly settled to the bottom than that which lay below the busiest ocean seaway.[5]

Thus, again in *Science*,[6] two Ivy League professors, John Zeller Imbrie of Brown and James Douglas Hays of Columbia, along with Cambridge don Sir Nicholas John Shackleton (1937–2006), combined to examine the record of deep sea deposits. They mostly focused the part of the Indian Ocean farthest from any significant land mass and most likely to hold a record of deposits unaffected by regional outwash from riverine activity, so as to have the cleanest record of what isotopes of which element were actually dropping from the skies and landing in the open ocean. In the summary of their lengthy article, which was entitled "Variations in the Earth's Orbit: Pacemaker of the Ice Ages,"[7] they found much agreement with Milankovitch, as follows:

1. Three indices of global climate have been monitored in the record of the past 450,000 years in Southern Hemisphere ocean-floor sediments.
2. Over the frequency range $10^{-4}$ to $10^{-5}$ cycles per year, climatic variance of these records is concentrated in three distinct peaks at periods of 23,000, 42,000, and approximately 100,000 years. These peaks correspond to the dominant periods of Earth's solar orbit and contain about 10, 25, and 50 percent of the climatic variance, respectively.
3. The 42,000-year climatic component has the same period as variations in the obliquity of Earth's axis and retains a constant phase relationship with it.
4. The 23,000-year portion of the variance displays the same periods (about 23,000 and 19,000 years) as the quasi-periodic precession index.
5. The dominant 100,000-year climatic component has an average period close to, and is in phase with, orbital eccentricity. Unlike the correlations between climate and the higher-frequency orbital variations, which can be explained on the assumption that the climate system responds linearly to orbital forcing, an explanation of the correlation between climate and eccentricity probably requires an assumption of nonlinearity.
6. It is concluded that changes in Earth's orbital geometry are the fundamental cause of the succession of quaternary ice ages.
7. A model of future climate based on the observed orbital-climate relationships, but *ignoring anthropogenic effects*[8] (emphasis added), predicts that the long-term trend over the next several thousand years is toward extensive Northern Hemisphere glaciation.

That one emphasized phrase is the scariest caveat in their entire report, and it leads to the unhappy finish of the final chapter. We know that man was able to evolve and thrive in the glacial epochs of the Pleistocene era, but we apparently will not, or cannot, evolve fast enough to survive the warming effects from all that carbon dioxide we are loading — more and more every day — into Earth's atmosphere due to our collective and willful short-sightedness, laziness, and greed. Human knowledge, but not human morality, is moving at a pace far faster that even most scientists recognize, as well as our societal ability to rationalize and control all that knowledge.

Human knowledge — as represented by scientific discoveries of all sorts, especially in communications — has increased by leaps and bounds at an ever-accelerating rate in the past century. However, our collective ability to restrain the many antisocial applications of some of these discoveries appears to have not advanced very much at all, thus putting all forms of life on the entire planet in some sort of danger. Precisely what (or which) kind of danger remains to be seen, but the possibilities are scarily enormous. Perhaps, as in the phrase that the great modern satirist Pogo is alleged to have coined, "We have met the enemy, and he is us."

In the thirty-volume twentieth-century edition of the *Encyclopedia Britannica,* published in 1906 by the Werner Company of Akron, Ohio, one can read of many things, but the totality of that obviously great mass of knowledge is but a small fraction of that which became available to anyone with a computer barely one century — and numerous wars and epidemics — later. The human race is facing a lot more trouble than was believed by the wisest folk that could be found in 1906.

# VIII
# Evolution?

*We see in this the evidence that man has been a long time learning to write history, but has been making history for many thousands and perhaps tens of thousands of years.*

— William F. Libby, Nobel Lecture (1960)

This chapter is our only portion that is likely to smack of argument, but the words (forthcoming) of Edward Wilber Berry (1875–1945) are so eloquent and sensible that any opus of this sort would be embarrassingly incomplete without something of this nature. Berry, who died in office as the widely respected president of the Geological Society of America, started out his adult career at various occupations in his native New Jersey, until he found satisfactory employment as a newspaper writer, by which time he had also become an ardent amateur student of nature. In due course, he turned professional, and after the age of thirty, was largely associated with the paleontological subset of geology and Johns Hopkins University, where he became one of that institution's leading intellectual lights and a frequent contributor to scientific journals. Among his most notable contributions to understanding is the article he composed for *The Scientific Monthly*, in August of 1922, entitled "The Geologic Evidence of Evolution." This entire article is so clearly and eloquently written that it deserves a more massive treatment than we have given to our previous cited authors. The major excerpts that follow are also as informative and scientifically valid, nearly a century later, as when first written.

> One of the outstanding, possibly the only difference between man and the other animals, is his ability to profit by the experience and accumulated

wisdom of the race, and yet, despite this characteristic, each generation seems to produce its quota of anti-vaccinationists, anti-evolutionists and believers in a flat earth. We may still entertain the hope that the race is becoming more rational when we recall that it has taken about three centuries to convince the Anglo-Saxon and a few other races among the countless millions of the globe that the earth is not flat …

I do not wish to be thought of as sneering at any one's beliefs, and I fully realize that there are a great many earnest Christian men and women who are perturbed at anything they think, rightly or wrongly, will shake the foundations of their faith, who are puzzled by the present outspoken opposition to evolution, and who wish to know what is the truth. No truer article of faith was ever penned than the motto of the Johns Hopkins[1] University — *Veritas Vos Liberabit* — and to you seekers after truth I would like to explain away certain misconceptions, before undertaking to show you that the record of earth history is the record of evolution, and not to be disputed by honest people.

Evolution is not a theory of origins, nor an article of scientific faith, but an indisputable fact. We could not teach geology without teaching evolution. One of the difficulties to the layman is the confusion of evolution — the record of the past and present history of organisms — with various theories that have been proposed to explain its factors or modes of operation. Let me emphasize that evolution, the record, is in an altogether different category from the theories such as Darwinism, Lamarckianism,[2] or any other ism that has been advanced to explain its workings. You may flout all the theories or you may advocate one of a dozen different theories, but this has nothing to do with the history of life. We, in geology, spend much time in going over the history of organisms, but pay slight attention to the theories — at least in our teaching.[3]

A simple illustration of the once universal and now fortunately less frequent clerical reaction to evolution will make clear what I am driving at. Evolution was regarded as a dangerous heresy, inimical to Christianity, contrary to Genesis, which was regarded as a scientific account of the origin of the earth and its inhabitants. Do these people claim that the hundreds of varieties of horses, dogs, chickens and pigeons go back to the garden of Eden, or were in Noah's ark, or that all the horticultural varieties of flowers, shrubs and vegetables were in Mother Eve's kitchen garden? Not at all! They are more or less familiar with the cattle breeders or the Burbank method of artificial selection. Their objection to evolution rests on the assumption that man is of a different stuff from the brute world — as if they had had no experience with congregations or legislative assemblies. It is the implied relationship with monkeys, and the tradition engendered by medieval art that the devil has a tail that offends their dignity.

The statement that the human species is descended from monkeys is merely polemical obscurantism and the playing on prejudices that started with Bishop Wilberforce — soapy Sam[4] as he was called by some of his contemporaries — and is a sort of Bryanesque smoke screen. As to lineage, man is not at all closely related to existing monkeys or apes. They are the culmination of different lines of evolution, and this statement is especially true of the monkeys. That their ancestry in the far distant past approximated the human line or indeed may have merged with it millions of years ago in early Tertiary times is quite another matter.

I find nothing in Genesis either for or against evolution. The language, to be sure, is not explicit (dust of the earth), but the special creation of man as opposed to the evolutionary creation is entirely an egotistical interpretation that is supposed, quite wrongly it seems to me, to add dignity to ourselves, and is of a cloth with the idea that the earth is the center of the universe — all the earth homocentric [centering on Man] and all the Universe revolving around Earth — man's temporary abode. It is a most curious revelation in the workings of the human mind that so many good people grow indignant over the idea that man was made from a long line of animal ancestry, as degrading; and yet who do not quarrel with the facts that each human starts his or her individual life as a single cell, and during the nine months preceding birth passes through a series of stages that roughly approximate the main stages of evolution, even to possessing a rudimentary tail like an ape. Five hundred years ago we should have said that embryology was the invention of the devil to test the faith of the elect — exactly a reason that was once advanced to explain the fossils in the rocks. Today most of us know better, and we find in the truth of creation far more to reverence than in the anthropomorphic deity of the childhood of the races.

In approaching the geological record of evolution, I will state only facts and leave fundamental causes severely alone. The mechanism of evolution we leave to experimental biology, and I do not advocate any theories of explanation. Here is evolution. Here are the myriad of forms that moved across the stage of the past and were the actors in the drama of life. In geology, to borrow a simile from written history of philology, we are dealing with the original documents insofar as they were preserved as fossils, and in the actual order of succession.

In approaching the geological record, the time conception is most important, and I can best illustrate this by a brief recital of the progress of knowledge concerning fossils. It is only in comparatively modern times that fossils have been recognized as the remains of animals and plants that had once been alive. The early Greeks were sane enough to recognize this apparently obvious relationship, and we find Xenophanes, in 500 BCE, speculating on the fossils found in the quarries of Syracuse, Sicily. But during the Middle Ages there was no end of discussion regarding the nature and origin of fossils. What seems strange in this year of grace may really not have been so strange in the days when the universally held belief was that of spontaneous generation, a flat earth created in six days, and the only past submergence of the land [was] that of Noah's flood. Was it not the same "plastic force" in nature which traced the frost patterns and the moss agate that fashioned the fossils, and was there not every gradation from shells and bones that exactly resemble recent ones to mere stones of similar form and appearance? We now know that the mineral replaces the organic matter of a fossil. Was it strange to have believed three of four hundred years ago that the process was the reverse — from the mineral to the organic? At any rate many strange theories were evolved to explain the fossils. One tells us that fossil shells were formed on the hills by the influence of the stars. Others called up a stone-making spirit. Others believed that fossils were the models made by the Creator in perfecting his work before he essayed the task of making living organisms. I am quoting entirely the views of devout churchmen. Others believed that fossils were mere "figured stones," or were the abortive products of the germs of animals and plants that had lost their way in the earth, or that they were inventions of the devil to test their faith. Even after the belief that fossils were the remains of animals and plants had become well established, it was assumed they had been killed by Noah's flood and stranded on mountain tops — an interpretation suggested by Martin Luther in 1539 as secular proof of the correctness of the scriptural account. This flood theory found numerous advocates throughout the seventeenth and even far into the eighteenth century. It passed through various phases of opinion. At first the fossils were regarded as similar to those still living in the vicinity — a natural enough belief when the universal acceptance of the Mosaic cosmology and a world but 6,000 years old is borne in mind. Later, when the differences in fossils became apparent, it was assumed that they had been swept to Europe and buried by the waters of the flood and represented forms still existing in the tropics. With the progress of knowledge of tropical organisms, this last view became untenable, and it was thought that the fossils represented forms that had been exterminated by the flood, and from this it was but a slight step to the once popular belief that there had been no thistles or weeds or noxious insects in the Garden of Eden, that all creation had become base with the fall of man. Gradually it came to be recognized that fossils were not only frequently unlike recent organisms, but that they were very ancient, not merely antediluvian, but pre-Adamic — a view first advanced by Blumenbach[5] in 1790. We are still far from a chronology. Granting that fossils were the traces of once living organisms and antedated Adam — what of it? When Guettard[6] made one of the first geological maps, it wasn't really a geological map in the modern sense, but a map of what he called mineral bands (like a modern soil map). He had no idea of geological succession or of structure. The credit of recognizing fossils as the modals of creation we owe to the genius of William Smith (1769–1839)[7] and to the orderly arrangement of the Mesozoic rocks of the English Midlands. Smith journeyed about for years in this region where the succession of fossiliferous strata is an open book. In his work of building canals, roads and drains, he observed that each bed contained fossils, some of which were peculiar to it, and he found that he could recognize the same horizons and the same succession at many different localities.

This important generalization has since been verified and endlessly extended. The contained fossils furnish the surest guides to the age of the sedimentary rocks that geology knows. To the biologist these facts have a deeper meaning, for they show that during the vast lapse of time, to be measured in tens or hundreds of millions of years, the living population of the globe has undergone almost continuous change, old simple forms becoming extinct, and newer, more specialized, forms taking their place, the change being, in general, from lower to higher, in other words — evolution.

That God rested from his six days' task of creation, just 4004 years BC is so absurd that I have yet to meet a person of normal mind who believes in Archbishop Ussher's chronology.[8] There have been many attempts to determine the age of the earth in years — calculations of the rate of cooling of molten bodies, the rate of retardation by tidal friction, the

> thickness of the sedimentary rocks, the amount of dissolved salts added to the oceans by the rivers of the world, the condition of radium minerals in igneous rocks. All methods contain unknown variables and are merely estimates. A favorite method has been to measure the thickness of a composite section of the sedimentary rocks, for the whole record is not complete in any one section — seas and sediments shifted with the incessant change in geographic pattern. If they had not, we should have such a perfect record of evolution with no missing chapters that we should be able to establish geological time boundaries between rock formations or biological boundaries between animal and plant groups.

Berry, who studied an enormous variety of paleobotanical remnants ranging from Indian Head, Maryland, across the broad Mississippi basin to the deserts of eastern Oregon, went on — for several more pages — to explain the evolution of horses and other familiar animals, concluding with that of man. In 1960, nearly forty years after Berry's essay was written, explorations of fossil remnants in the Olduvai Gorge area of mid-Africa did nothing to amend the substance of his findings, nor have any discoveries since that date.

In summing up, this erudite expositor noted:

> The rest of the [Earth's] history belongs more to Anthropology and Archeology. The Robenhausian[9] culture of the Swiss and other lake dwellings about 7000 BCE shows permanent lake dwellings, domestication of animals and cultivation of crops with use of pottery; the Copper Age extended from 3000 to 2000 BCE ; the Bronze Age in Europe from about 2000 to 1000 BCE, in the Orient from 4000 to 1800 BCE; the Iron Age (earlier or Hallstatt[10] culture) in Europe from 1000 to 500 BCE; in the Orient from 1800 to 1000; and the latter Iron Age from 500 BCE to Roman times in Europe. Note the cumulative rapidity of the advance as compared with slowness of change in earlier stages.
>
> Although very much remains to be discovered, we know enough to assure the layman that man has had a long evolutionary history, extending over tens if not hundreds of thousands of years. Does this knowledge breed cynicism and irresponsibility? What answer does science give on this point? Since late Paleolithic time, i.e., toward the close of the Old Stone Age, 25,000 years ago, man's biological evolution has been slight and to some extent retrograde. Skull, bones and teeth have changed but little. It was during this period of slight physical change

> that our race has made astonishing progress, and the hope is natural that there is no limit to the betterment of the race by the exercise of wisdom, altruism and idealism — the spiritual graces if you choose so to call them.

• • •

It has long been noted by seismologists (both Jesuit and lay) and other students of reality that the careful timing of the reception of different types of earthquake waves traveling by separate paths through the interior of this planet was a means whereby precise determination could be made of where a seismic event had occurred — as well as how severe it was. While, like all of us, these folk are perched on the outer solid fringe of the planet on which all life (along with its many inflated egos) exist, they have thus been able to also deduce from these shock waves that the inner core of Earth is likely composed of a very hot, very dense, iron- and cobalt-rich, and probably highly magnetic mass. These inner attributes of our planet, in addition, manifest themselves in the orientation of the compass and the behavior of some elements of the Sun's radiation as its rays impact the outer parts of Earth's atmosphere.

James Alfred Van Allen (1914–2006), an Iowa-born physicist, is credited with the identification of a series of radiation belts surrounding planet Earth, outside the well-known ozone layer. Among other attributes, these belts serve to protect Earth from some of the radiations, mostly solar, that are inimical to life on Earth. As a significant consultant to the National Aeronautic and Space Administration, he theorized on the existence of these protective shields and their interaction with the cosmic rays that apparently fill the universe beyond.

NASA thereupon set out to probe these belts to determine what earthly uses could be made of near-space that would not interfere with what seemed to be a very protective arrangement for all the life on Earth. Thus comes the name for the Van Allen Belts, a heavenly area of protective shielding that saves all Earthlings from immediately succumbing to what might otherwise be compared to high-level microwave cooking.

The most recent emanations from NASA indicate there are three such belts, at varying distances above Earth, and they are all very much influenced by solar storms and other irregularities coming from our parent Sun. These belts, however, are far beyond the outer limits of Earth's atmosphere and are not likely to be affected by the deleterious pollution that man is inserting into our air — more and more every day. The living creatures that inhabit Earth have little to fear from any damage we can do to the Van Allen belts, but a great deal to fear from the damage we are inflicting a good bit closer to home.

Recent visitors to Europe have observed the extent to which classical marble statues, such as adorn many of the scenic villas of Italy — some as young as two centuries old — are suffering (severely discolored[11] and literally rotting apart) from the increasingly bad air that is endemic due to industrial pollution in the valley of the Po River. Italy is not alone in experiencing this problem; China is now notorious, but every industrial (First World) nation is part of the problem. Not one nation (or faction) has taken a leading position in seeking to be a part of the solution.

• • •

Sir John Scott Haldane (1860–1936) studied the effect of gaseous poisoning of coal miners, as well as the nature of the toxic gasses used by both the German and the Allied Armies in the Great War. In 1911, he headed a scientific party that went to the top of Pikes Peak (via both road and railway) to study the effects of lower air pressure on the human anatomy, a special subset of medicine of which the leading light in recent years became Dr. Charles Snead Houston (1913–2009), an American alpinist and physiologist of great note. As noted by both the critics of Sergeant O'Keeffe and the employees of Professor Pickering, this exalted locale becomes a busy place for research every so often.

However, it remained for Sir Joseph Barcroft (1872–1947), another British research physiologist and chemist known mostly for his studies on the oxygenation of blood, to carry this matter to a finer level of understanding, though he became highly regarded as the principal British student of the most used wartime toxic gas (chlorine) in 1915. A devout Quaker, he was also widely respected for his frequent practice of using himself as a guinea pig for his own risky studies. Of interest, however, in the context of this opus, are the findings his team reported as a result of their 1922 expedition to the Peruvian Andes, where they made careful studies of the physiological adjustments and development of those Peruvian Incas who had lived — at least since the Spanish conquest early in the sixteenth century — at altitudes exceeding 14,000 feet.[12] This is a significantly different environment from the great bulk of the human species, which lives well below 1,000 feet above sea level, and for the most part, does not ever leave this "high-pressure" environment. In studying these Incas, Barcroft learned that the lung capacity of these particular humans was far greater than that of "normal" *Homo sapiens* — like himself — who live, reproduce, and evolve (?) at much lower altitudes.

Ang Tshering Sherpa at the 2013 meeting in Pontresina, Switzerland, of the International Association of Alpine Clubs. With the burly physique typical of his "tribe," Ang Tsering is a modern leader in Nepalese and world alpinism. *W. L. Putnam III.*

Since it was another area of special interest to this physiologist, he also inquired about the customs — taboos — pertinent to pregnancy among those Inca descendants in Peru. In pursuing this topic, Sir Joseph and his team found that, though the females among his test subjects had also developed a similarly greater lung capacity, there was a taboo among them that specified, during the last trimester of any pregnancy, a woman was required to go down to a lower-level valley until she delivered her child.

Dr. Buddha Basnyat, a globally respected physician and physiologist of Kathmandu (and one of this scribe's closer friends), has noted the higher lung capacity among his Sherpa neighbors who now live in Nepal. Over uncounted generations, these folk developed the greater lung capacity needed for effective oxygenation of the blood at high altitude, for the Sherpas (now of Nepal) were originally natives of Tibet — where their collective name means "the East people." Many of the Han Chinese now living in Tibet practice the same altitude-based taboos as the Incas, particularly the one regarding pregnancy.

However, according to Dr. Basnyat, the Sherpas have been at it for a great deal longer than the upland Incas of the Andes. In moving to Nepal, however, as a result of being evicted from their homeland, the Sherpas were going from a domicile at a higher altitude to one that is somewhat lower. Yet as in all such taboos, there is an element of tradition, or religion, about it that derives from ancient practical lore that is seldom fully understood in the present day.[13] The Sherpas, however, by the gradual elimination of those who did not share this common attribute — of great value in high, thin air — have also developed a societal "hypoxia inducible gene" (Dr. Basnyat's term), presumably as a result of their untold prior generations living at a much higher altitude, a gene that — as far as we know at this date — seems not to be in play (or at least not to be active) among the high-altitude Incas. This unique gene alone may give the Sherpas their now traditional major leg up over those who have the means to hire them to help ascend the world's highest peaks.[14]

In these two so-called primitive societies, the practical result of violating such taboos was so often fatal that the taboo took on a quasi-religious nature and thus became emotionally inviolable. Regardless of how this attribute came about, it becomes clear that many of God's creatures — and very likely man as well, as noted by researchers from Friar Mendel through Luther Burbank and Edward Berry to Dr. Basnyat — can evolve to different specifications by the very simple process of eliminating from the collective gene pool those who violate the taboos by their failure to reproduce. In other words, this is the survival of those fittest to live in the evolving environment. Darwin had noted this adaptive condition among the beak dimensions of the various finches that lived on isolated parts of the Galapagos Islands, and it started him thinking about how long it took for some of the adaptations required to become integral to survival of the species. It turned out to be only a couple of generations among finches, since those who had the wrong-shaped beaks simply starved to death before they could partake of the birds' annual rite of reproduction.

If some of us have similar means to survive the "toasting" process that appears to be our future, *Homo sapiens* may well be in for a comparable evolution. But don't bet on it; the lucky ones will probably be accused of witchcraft and then killed by their jealous neighbors.

• • •

A prime example of readily accepted evolution is the progress of understanding the varied realities about the bubonic plague, which famously devastated all of Europe as the Black Death in the fifteenth century. At the time, no one knew where it came from or how it spread; the disease was blamed on various evil practices — often not much different from those that had so disappointed the Almighty God a few thousand years earlier and led to the building of Noah's ark. People sought countless means to avoid developing the "buboes" (lymph node swellings) that characterized the deadly disease in humans. The progress of this widespread affliction, striking the rich and the poor, the holy and the unholy alike, was recorded by European journalists ranging from Boccaccio to Pepys. But at the time, no one understood how it spread from place to place and person to person. One only seemed to escape it by burning all one's possessions, fleeing to places with fresh air, and living a simple and outdoorsy life; and even that was unsuccessful for quite a few of those who succumbed.

In time — several centuries of it — people learned, by careful observation of pertinent facts, that this affliction had started in China in the mid-fourteenth century, was spread across Asia on the Silk Road (north of the Himalayan/Karakoram ranges) by merchants and other travelers to the Black Sea, and thence brought to Sicily by Italian seamen and traders. From Italy, it soon spread to every country of Europe, but no one knew how, except that the symptoms suddenly appeared and death often followed within twenty-four hours — initially in port cities.

It was not until the mid-nineteenth century that researchers finally put all the pertinent facts together in a logical and easy-to-comprehend manner. Bubonic plague obviously traveled by both land and sea; it went readily from fleas to rats and thence from fleas to humans. Now, in the twenty-first century, we know that certain drugs provide a rapid cure and that cleanliness and avoidance of fleas and infected rodents is an equally good measure to avoid the plague.

*Job hath spoken without knowledge, and his words were without wisdom.*

— Job, 34:35 (KJB)

*Therefore doth Job open his mouth in vain; he multiplieth words without knowledge.*

— Job, 25:16(KJB)

*Facta canam; sed erunt qui*
*me finxisse loquantur.*

*I will sing of facts; but there will be*
*some to say I have invented them.*

— Publius Ovidius Naso (43 BCE–17 AD)
Book VI, Ch 3

Great Barrier Reef, Queensland, Australia

IX

# What's Next?

*For whom he did foreknow, he also did predestinate to be conformed.*
— Romans 8:29 (KJB)

It might be more appropriate for someone who has a flair, or a name, for science-fiction writing to compose this final word, for it is a safe bet that there will be some presently unthought, bizarre, futuristic, unheard-of, or downright heroic measures taken during man's final days — before our God finally turns this planet over to the cockroaches, who seem to be immune to any form of pestilence or other means of extinction.

There are precious few points on which all knowledgeable authorities appear to be unanimous, but nevertheless, there is one. It is already severe and probably beyond repair, but any further increase in the carbon dioxide content of Earth's atmosphere is bound to (1) cause greater global warming, (2) hence resulting in faster melting of the world's remaining glaciers, (3) thus raising sea level and reducing the amount of habitable land, (4) thereby also bringing on a greater severity of weather — not necessarily warmer weather, but definitely more severe in every way: thunderstorms, blizzards, tornados, hurricanes, typhoons, heat waves, floods, and that ilk — (5) thereby crowding us ever closer into that social chaos that many seers have predicted will arrive just prior to the final battle of mankind at Armageddon.[1] Indeed, within the current human life span, it has been possible to note some validity to such a contention. In her one hundredth year, this scribe's mother (1892–1993) commented that she felt the "equinoctial storms" (her words) of her youth were not nearly as severe as those hurricanes she could more frequently see raging outside her window in Massachusetts.

Furthermore, studies of laboratory rats (the albino version of *Rattus norvegicus*) have found, among other things, that when allowed sufficient personal space, white rats get along with each other in tolerable equanimity. But when closely crowded, they lose this innate sense of personal responsibility and lapse into all manner of antisocial behavior. Are we seeing signs of that process among *Homo sapiens* today? Hmm!

• • •

In mid-March of the year 1888, a severe blizzard struck the American Northeast, depositing snowdrifts up to twenty feet high, closing all communications, curtailing railroad traffic for weeks, and so affecting normal life that one New Yorker, trapped while visiting friends in Boston, felt obligated to send a telegram via two transatlantic cables through London to assure his relatives in Manhattan that he was safe and not to be presumed stuck on some train in one of those twenty-foot drifts in southern New England. The storm was a shocker and drew much criticism to the U.S. Weather Bureau, then under the charge of Signal Service Major General Adolphus Washington Greely (1844–1935). However, his meteorologists had tracked the disturbance as it crossed the continent and did predict a major snowstorm, but they were betrayed by an unusual preseasonal strengthening of the Bermuda High that unexpectedly stalled the disturbance just off the south coast of New England and kept it swirling in place for an extended forty-eight hours.

More modern and more complete weather monitoring of a century and a quarter later (including previously unconsidered variations in Pacific Ocean surface water temperatures, and the knowledge and tracking of upper-level highs and lows) has allowed such recent disturbances to be predicted with greater accuracy. But since man can seldom be completely

The infamous "Blizzard of '88" shut down most of the Northeast for days following March 13, 1888, including the main rail and telegraph lines south of Boston.

sure of what lies beyond human view — no matter how sophisticated that view — there are still bound to be some unpleasant surprises, and we can surely count on their appearance, even if we do not wish them to occur. But mankind — indeed this whole planet — has never had to deal with the results of the massive change man has collectively wrought, bit by bit and ever so slowly over the past two or three centuries, in the atmosphere that we breathe and that generates the detailed weather and the whole ecosystem that every living creature also calls home. This stricture pertains even to those residing under the ocean surface, for it too has simultaneously become alarmingly more acidic.

The process has been slow to become appreciated in greatest part because it has been so gradual. Had it come on us like the squall line of a vigorous cold front, we might have seen it differently, but the approach of doom has been sneaky. Those glaciers that were so large a century ago didn't disappear overnight (poof!); they slowly and quietly melted away. The air samples that scientists have analyzed from time to time didn't develop into incipient toxicity overnight. They got scary ever so gradually that no one became suddenly alarmed at the crisis most educated folk know we now face. Humanity's condition is somewhat comparable to the idea of boiling a frog. If you toss the critter into a pot that is already boiling, he is so shocked that he jumps out immediately and is saved; but if you put him in a bucket of cold water and then gradually raise the temperature, the frog will be slow-cooked before he becomes fully aware of his changing environment.

Compounding the changes man has unintentionally brought to our planet is the indisputable fact that there are ever more of our species, all continuously demanding a higher standard of living, and thus more earthly resources. Every aspect of modern man's economy is based on exceeding the production and consumption records of each prior year. At some point — for Earth is finite — we will be forced to accept the fact that there is indeed a Malthusian limit to the Biblical mandate to "increase and multiply."[2] Unfortunately, according to many astronomical and climatological scientists, we have already passed that limit, and it is too late to turn back. Much to be regretted, however, is the fact that Christian and other religious leaders — in association with numerous seemingly uneducatable politicians — are unperturbed and intent, as has traditionally been the case, on simply denying the merit in any facts they do not wish to face. They still call for the production of ever more souls "for the greater glory of God in the next world," regardless of what sort of quality of life, if any at all, planet Earth can be expected to afford the bodies pertinent to those souls as they transit this world en route to that hopefully glorious next world.

• • •

The immortal and ubiquitous cockroach — inheritor of planet Earth? *W. L. Putnam III.*

There is also room for a less gloomy possibility. Current trends among First World nations, as well as individual members of higher-education-level families everywhere, show a decline in birth rate that appears to be related to the desire to get more out of this life than the mere hope for a better one later — as promised for millennia by religious leaders of all stripes. The fact that this trend is also somewhat related to income is not nearly as strong as that such an outlook on life is related to education. It shows that an educated person is more likely to be unafraid to throw off the quasi-hypnotic yoke of generational shamanism in any of its manifestations. If this possibility becomes the way of the future soon, then maybe there *is* a future.

Equally possible, though far less likely, is the hope that the people of democratic nations will soon cease electing to high office those who appeal to their baser instincts through denial of fact, encouragement of short-range greed, happy ignorance, and hedonism. Instead, they will hopefully elect those with sufficient fortitude and knowledge to forcefully set both personal and national economies to lower expectations with (1) vastly less economic reliance on a never-ending increase of human population, and (2) discontinued overuse of fossil fuels — for it is the press of human numbers that will soon crowd us out of food supplies and the excessive use of fossil fuels that has driven the atmospheric issue of the greenhouse effect.

The Reverend Malthus may have been proven wrong in 1798, because humanity has avoided the trouble he predicted by ever greater use of fossil fuels. But when the air becomes "uraneous," or intolerably hot for all mammals, the increasingly acidic oceans begin to boil, and we arrive closer to a "standing room only" condition for this planet, he is bound to have been right. All serious climatologists predict — when not preaching about abject disaster from the warming of Earth's atmosphere — that weather of all sorts, both hot and cold, as well as wet and dry, will likely get more severe. There's just no other rational or scientifically predictable outcome.

For further reading — on an especially long or rainy weekend — we heartily recommend the 2011 book *Collapse!*[3] by Dr. Jared Mason Diamond, Professor of Geography at UCLA, from which we offer a few selections below. Dr. Diamond was concerned with smaller groups that could be identified within the totality of mankind. Herein this scribe deals with the whole shebang — every living thing on the face of the Earth, except, of course, the cockroaches:

> *Page 114, concerning the now treeless Easter Island, 2,000 miles from any other land in the southeast Pacific Ocean:*
> I have often asked myself, "What did the Easter Islander who cut down the last palm tree say while he was doing it?" Like modern loggers, did he shout "Jobs, not trees"? Or: "Technology will solve our problems, never fear, we'll find a substitute for wood"? Or: "We don't have proof that there aren't palms somewhere else on Easter, we need more research, your proposed ban on logging is premature and driven by fear-mongering." Similar questions arise for every society that has inadvertently damaged its environment.
>
> *Also page 119:*
> The Easter Islanders' isolation probably also explains why I have found that their collapse, more than the collapse of any other pre-industrial society, haunts my readers and students. The parallels between Easter Island and the whole modern world are chillingly obvious. Thanks to globalization, international trade, jet planes, and the Internet, all countries on Earth today share resources and affect each other, just as did Easter's dozen clans. Polynesian Easter Island was as isolated in the Pacific Ocean as the Earth is today in Space. When the Easter Islanders got into difficulties, there was nowhere to which they could flee, nor to which they could turn for help; nor shall we modern Earthlings have recourse elsewhere if our troubles increase. Those are the reasons why people see the collapse of Easter Island society as a metaphor, a worst-case scenario, for what may lie ahead of us in our own future.[4]
>
> *Page 156, concerning Chaco Canyon:*
> The reason is that the initial conditions of abundant nearby trees, high groundwater levels, and a smooth flood plain without arroyos had disappeared.
>
> That type of conclusion is likely to apply to many other collapses of

> past societies (including the Maya to be considered in the next chapter), and to our own destiny today. All of us moderns — house-owners, investors, politicians, university administrators, and others — can get away with a lot of waste when the economy is good. We forget that conditions will change. By that time, we may have become attached to an expensive lifestyle, leaving an enforced diminished lifestyle or bankruptcy as the sole outs.
>
> *Page 159ff, concerning the Maya:*
> They did damage their environment, especially by deforestation and erosion. Climate changes (droughts) did contribute to the Maya collapse, probably repeatedly. Hostilities among the Maya themselves did play a large role. Finally, political/cultural factors, especially the competition among kings and nobles that led to a chronic emphasis on war and erecting monuments rather than on solving underlying problems, also contributed.
>
> *Also page 177:*
> Like Easter Island chiefs erecting ever larger statues, eventually crowned by pukao, and like the Anasazi elite treating themselves to necklaces of 2,000 turquoise beads, Maya kings sought to outdo each other with more and more impressive temples, covered with thicker and thicker plaster — reminiscent in turn of the extravagant conspicuous consumption by modern American CEOs. The passivity of Easter chiefs and Maya kings in the face of real big threats to their societies completes our list of disquieting parallels.

There is no easy way out! In the absence of any yet-to-be-observed collective and unanimously different lifestyle from that which "advanced" societies now take as "normal," as one of our contributors/advisors recently put it: "Before long, we're all toast!"[5]

On the other hand, the late Casey Stengel, another recent, diamond-based and often-cited philosopher of reality, has advised: "Never make predictions, especially about the future."

# Appendix of Comparisons

Some of the greatest mountain photographs ever taken are those by the justly admired Italian compositor Vittorio Sella (1859–1943), a nephew of Quintino Sella (1827–1884), one of the leaders of the Risorgimento movement[1] that reunited Italy in the mid-nineteenth century. The younger Sella's works are regarded today by most authorities as among the finest examples of mountain art ever produced. In 1897, he accompanied the famed Luigi Amedeo di Savoie/Aosta (1873–1933), known to all alpinists as the Duke of the Abruzzi, on several of his widely acclaimed expeditions.[2] These ranged from the first ascent of Alaska's Mount Saint Elias in 1897 to an attempt to attain the North Pole two years later (where a farthest north of 86°34′ was achieved by the Duke's second in command, Captain Umberto Cagni, in April of 1900), the first ascent of Africa's Rwenzori in 1906, and most famously, reconnoiter K2, the second-highest mountain of the world, in 1909.

Sella had also made several photographic expeditions to the Caucasus (Kafkas) in the years prior to joining the Duke's teams, on many of which trips he used 11" by 14" glass plates exclusively. Also, regularly accompanying the Duke's expeditions was his amanuensis and surgeon, Filippo de Filippi (1869–1938) of Turin, who authored several classic accounts that adorn the library shelves of many mountain bibliophiles.

In later years, many folk have attempted to duplicate some of the mountain pictures taken by Sella with occasional success. Many of these comparisons (some of the originals are now a century and more old) are available through the Decaneas Archives of Boston and are on exhibit in mountain museums around the world — of which the most complete are those of the Messner Mountain

Museum (Firmiani), set in a sometime-castle just outside Bolzano in the Alto Adige of North Italy.

We offer here copies of some of the Sella comparisons that are on finer display in that museum, along with others derived from lesser known alpinistic sources. A visit to Bolzano can easily be extended to see Ötsi,[3] the seven-thousand-year preserved iceman, whose remains were discovered in 1991 on the Schnalstal Glacier and can presently be found in equally cold storage at the Archeological Museum of South Tyrol, where he remains the subject of forensic research by scientists from around the world.

• • •

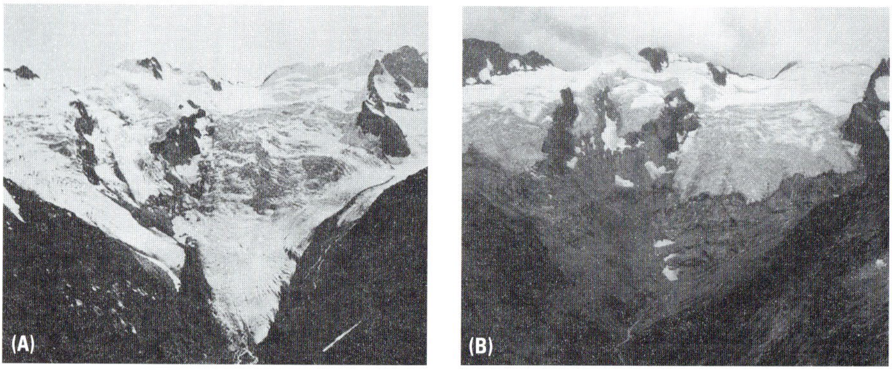


***The Battle Range of Canada***

(A) In 1914, two American exploratory alpinists, Minnesota's Professor Frederick King Butters (1878–1945) and the contemporary New York medical doctor Andrew James Gilmour, made the strenuous hike twenty miles south from the Glacier House to visit the quartz-monzonite peaks of the Battle Range, an area never before explored by mountaineers but that derived its unique name from a legendary contest of an unknown date between a prospector and a grizzly bear. The pair went south via a sometime trail in the valley of the Beaver River. They made the discovery of a large hanging lake and ascended a major peak, both of which were subsequently named for Professor Butters. In the course of this ascent, they looked south, across the valley of Butters Creek, to a glacier-hung series of secondary peaks subsequently known as the Schooner Ridge.

— *American Alpine Club, Gilmour photo*

(B) In 2013, ninety-nine years later, photographer and mountain guide Roger William Laurilla repeated that route, looked south, and noted the changes.

***A Century of Melting***

(A) In 1910, the late author, explorer, and alpinist Howard Palmer (1883–1944) of New London, Connecticut, went to nearly the crest of Azimuth Ridge in the Selkirk Range of British Columbia to establish a triangulation survey station, where he looked southwest and saw this scene, including the subpeak, Ravelin (at right). The combined Sir Sandford (lower center) and Silvertip Glaciers (even lower) then swept eastward (left) for another mile to its terminus. Note the narrow ridge of lateral moraine at the right (west) side of the Silvertip Glacier, holding back some snow and showing that the glacier had recently been even larger.

— *American Alpine Club, Howard Palmer*

(B) In 2010, the current Canadian writer, mountaineer, and scientist David Peter Jones went to almost the same spot as Palmer to look south-southwest and photograph the one-time junction point of the Silvertip Glacier with the larger Sir Sandford Glacier, of which a trace of its icefall remains. The tiny, silvery dot in the lower center is the Ben Ferris Hut of the Alpine Club of Canada, built in 1964, where there was over 400 feet of ice in 1910.

— *David. P. Jones*

• • •

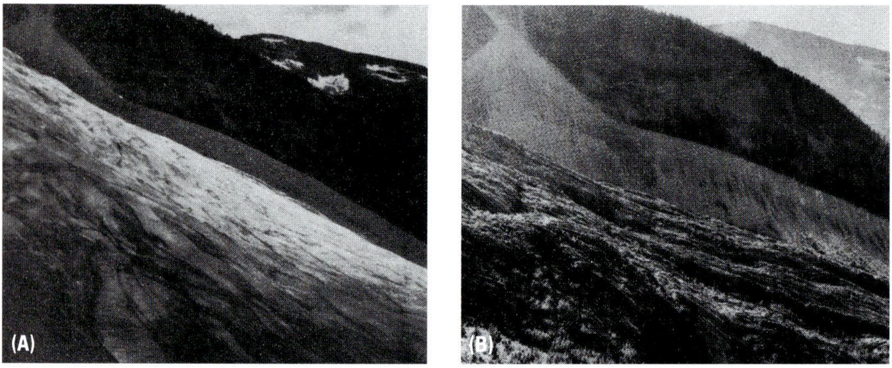


### *The (Not So) Great Glacier*

In 1982, the American Alpine Club published a volume entitled *The Great Glacier and Its House,* on page 85 of which appeared two pictures of the "great" Illecillewaet Glacier, both looking west from the same mid-level vantage point:

(A) A photo taken in 1892 shows the cascading glacier in full swing.

— *William Vaux*

(B) A picture from 1980 shows that, in what was its midcourse, the glacier is completely gone.

— *Roger W. Laurilla*

### *Switzerland*

This scribe obtained a picture postcard at a Swiss tourist trap near Brig showing the position of the Rhone Glacier (at the head of the river of the same name) at various landmark years in the past two centuries, ever since man (including the

Swiss) began intensive burning of fossil fuels — 1800, 1850, 1900, and 1950.

(A) The Formi Glacier, east of Bormio and south of the Stelvio Pass, was sketched by a local artist in about 1850 (and turned into a postcard).

— *Anonymous*

(B) More than a century and a half later (163 years to be exact), the same scene was visible — minus quite a bit of the glacier — from a delightful and scenic restaurant.

— *W. L. Putnam III*

• • •

***The Caucasus***

The natives of this, the highest mountain range of Europe, constructed sturdy towers as easily defended residences. This village was photographed in the late nineteenth century by a Royal Geographical Society team under the leadership of Douglas Freshfield, which included Sella. And after most of a century under the dominance of the repressive socialist regime of Stalinist Russia, it was also captured on film by Fabiano Ventura, a leading member of a second party of Italian alpinists, who visited the area as part of a reprise organized by Signor Silvio Calvi — alpinist, engineer, and architect of Bergamo.

— *J. Kent Robinson*

*Servant of God, well done; well hast thou fought the better fight, who single hast maintained against revolted multitudes the cause of truth*

— John Milton (1608–1674)
*Paradise Lost* VI – 1, 29

Victoria Falls, southern Africa

# Endnotes

**Introduction**

1. Elsewhere, verse 15 has been read as: "The perverse are hard to be corrected, and the number of fools is infinite."
2. Many of the place names of New England, and therefrom across the United States, reflect the affection of these Puritan forebears for the Roundhead landmarks of the conflict that resulted in Oliver Cromwell's rule as "Lord Protector" of Great Britain.
3. The ill-fated Armada, sent in 1588 from Spain and meant to bring the English leadership back into line with Rome, actually received a papal blessing — ostensibly for its religious implications and intentions. However, the original "insult" was done to a Spanish lady (Catherine of Aragon), though the blessing came from an Italian-born pope, Sixtus V.
4. This was also the year that the floundering Jamestown colony in Virginia had to be reinforced militarily; Henry Hudson died; Marco Antonio de Dominis (1566–1624), a sometime Italian prelate, published a scientific explanation of the rainbow; and King James's problems with the English Parliament began to intensify, ultimately leading to the dethronement and execution of his son, Charles.
5. Being an archbishop ran in the family; his father, Henry, had been the Church of Ireland's archbishop of Dublin.
6. There are two separate accounts of Creation in Genesis.
7. There are other authoritative Christian Bibles, such as those issued under the imprimatur of the Catholic Church — *Douai* and *Jerusalem* — but they do not differ in fundamental, "factual" content.
8. Since 1930, this process has been temporarily, and only somewhat, hindered by the construction of a series of dams — Senator Wash, Palo Verde, Imperial, Davis, Laguna, Hoover, Glen Canyon, and more, though the wildest part of the Canyon is still a favorite haunt of white-water rafters.
9. After all, most (Eurocentric) histories tell us that the New World was not even "discovered" until 1492 CE and still thought to be part of the Old World for some years afterward.

10. The ancient Greeks had a different solution for the presence of some later unwanted fellow travelers with Noah. They blamed the presence of various evils that appeared in human society during later years on a curious young lady named Pandora. There is, however, no evidence of theistic belief emanating from the more recent Olduvai Gorge discoveries in Tanganyika, so that concept must likely have come in later. When that happened remains a great question.
11. Between those two railroads were the Erie, which ran on New York City time, and the Pennsylvania, which ran on Philadelphia time. After the numerous bankruptcies and consolidations that came over American (but not Canadian) railways after the 1950s, it was no longer true that "a pig can cross the continent without changing stations in Chicago but a person cannot."

**Chapter I**

1. A term derived from the Swiss-French for a small, glacially polished bedrock outcrop.
2. A great number of Americans are of Germanic descent, a process that started in the early nineteenth century.
3. Funded under the will of John Lowell Jr. (1799–1836), a very successful merchant/ship owner of Boston who died in Mumbai, this unique, self-perpetuatingly managed institute is now charged with providing support for adult public education in Massachusetts and has thereby (through local PBS affiliate WGBH) become a major source of support for public television in the United States.
4. The full texts of these lectures, delivered in December 1848 through January 1849, are available in a reprint edition sponsored by the University of Michigan Library.
5. Lester G. Crocker, ed., *Diderot's Selected Writings* (New York: Macmillan, 1966).
6. These would be some of the improbable events associated by legend with Jonah, Moses, and Noah. Our OED has a somewhat different definition of "miracle," but to us, the word applies to any event for which the onlookers can supply no logical explanation.
7. Holy Scripture also tells us that quite a number of other natural disasters had hit Egypt in the years prior to 1490 BCE.
8. Katabatic winds are a camper's delight in the mountains. When this scribe was a young alpinist, exploring the "wrong" valleys in the mountains of Western Canada, he would try to find summer campsites just below a glacier or ample snowfield, where the air would cool during the night, gain weight, and descend, thereby driving the pesky mosquitoes away.

**Chapter II**

1. Alfred Lothar Wegener (1880–1930), a German meteorologist and geomorphologist, did most of his field work in Greenland, prior to the Great War of 1914–1918. Two world wars later, John Tuzo Wilson (1908–1993), the geologist son of a noted Canadian alpiniste, developed more convincing proof of the theory of plate tectonics and is regarded as the modern father of such studies.
2. *Plusça change ...* When this scribe was a student of geology, in the 1940s (under

the likes of Kirtley Fletcher Mather, Marland Pratt Billings, Cornelius Hurlbut, and Kirk Bryan), if one espoused the concept of continental drift, one was labeled as "some kind of nut who doesn't belong in geology." Now, if one does *not* explain major tectonic events by that mechanism, one soon becomes labeled as "some kind of nut who doesn't belong in geology."

3. The American battleship USS *Maine*, which famously capsized into the mud of Havana harbor on February 15, 1898, was later patched up, raised, towed out to sea, and resunk, descending 600 feet in the Florida Straits on March 16, 1912.
4. The roster of eminent seismologists reads somewhat like a litany of members of the Society of Jesus, one of the newest of the Catholic Church's many formalized religious orders, whose members are frequently notable authorities in several other scientific disciplines.
5. The Hawaiian Islands, though all of volcanic origin, become increasingly young and active, volcanically, as one moves to the east-southeast.
6. Chief Mountain, where this evidence was most effectively noted, is very visible from near the U.S.-Canadian border line on Interstate 15.
7. This must have been a doozy! The exploding debris spread thickly, as yellow-orange ash, well into southern British Columbia and Alberta, and eastward into central Montana.
8. The sound of the Krakatoa explosion was heard more than fifty miles away; and on its centenary, this scribe's mother, who was born in 1892, insistently recalled the brilliant sunsets of her youth.
9. One is reminded of the hoary lumber-camp story concerning a diminutive itinerant who approached the wangan boss, asking for a job as a faller. The boss told him to be gone, but the itinerant persisted until the employer finally gave in, asking the little man to drop a tree, obviously leaning the other way, right at the boss's feet. The little man walked over to the tree and around it several times, and then made an appropriate notch with his chain saw. Crash! The tree fell just as asked, greatly impressing the potential hirer.

   "Where'd you learn to drop a tree like that?" he inquired.

   "In the Sahara," replied the little man.

   "But that's a @#$%& desert," rejoined the boss.

   "Well, it is *now*!"
10. These sources also represent a sort of global energy savings bank. But atomic energy is not fully immune from this criticism, for in the end, it is yet another, merely more modern, heat-creating process — and one not requiring the burning of oxygen.
11. Eight months later (August 7, 2013) as this opus was in its end stages, the *Wall Street Journal* also carried an article on page 4, referenced on its front page, detailing certain facts on the recent global rise in sea level.
12. The Greeks made their pillars in segments (as shown in the temple ruins picture on page 27) that could be lifted into place atop each other and pinned by leaden pegs so as not to slide out of place. The Romans often made their columns of single units, which were then elevated in a manner similar to the ramp-and-rope techniques used by the Easter Islanders.
13. See Acts XX: 13–17. According to *The Oxford Bible Commentary*, the Acts were

largely compiled by the evangelist (and physician) Luke, who appears to have also accompanied Paul on this final voyage.

14. Polybius (200–118 BCE) is particularly noteworthy among historians for his emphasis on factuality in the recording of events.
15. Preparatory to assaulting Hitler's Gothic Line across the Northern Apennines, this scribe's unit of the United States 10th Mountain Division, bivouacked on a royal estate (now a national park) that lies south of Pisa on part of this delta.
16. We make no comment on the geomorphic or environmental folly of trying to maintain a major city below sea level and beside a river whose bottom is measurably higher than the streets of the city.
17. To quote Sherlock Holmes: "Elementary, my dear Watson."
18. Robert Jastrow, *God and the Astronomers*, 2nd ed. (New York: W. W. Norton & Company, 1992).
19. Lemaître was a diocesan priest, though his scientific acumen was such that many folk assumed he belonged to the Society of Jesus. Throughout its existence, that organization has had problems with authority, not merely temporal, as with many European monarchies, but even with some of the Popes. LeMaître's stature, however, was such that he was even tapped to preside over a papal commission to formulate policy on birth control.
20. For more on Ratti, see my book *The Mountaineer's Pontiff: Achille Ratti* (Authors House, 2006). No matter what one's nationality, it is a mark of arrival to be elected a regular member of the Alpine Club — a recognition of one's acceptance and accomplishment among mountaineers. Honorary membership is generally reserved for those who have also excelled at some other form of human endeavor.
21. For more on Slipher, consult the brief biography *Vesto Melvin Slipher* by William Graves Hoyt, published by the National Academy of Sciences in 1980.
22. The Mongol rulers of China even tried to conquer Japan in the thirteenth century but were defeated by a typhoon, as recounted by Ms. Jehuda Neumann in the *Bulletin of the American Meteorological Society* (November 1975).
    Arthur Quiller-Couch, The Oxford Book of English Verse: 1250–1900. Edward Fitzgerald (1809–1883), 698. From Omar Khayyám.
23. A Book of verses underneath the Bough,
    A jug of wine, a loaf of bread
    And Thou beside me singing in the Wilderness
    Edward Fitzgerald, "From Omar Khayyám," in the *Oxford Book of English Verse*, ed. Arthur Quiller-Couch (Oxford: Clarendon, 1919).
24. Younghusband (1863–1942) also visited V. M. Slipher in Flagstaff on March 3, 1914, noting, "I have immensely enjoyed my first look at the heavens through a big telescope."
25. Stein (1862–1943) was of Hungarian Jewish extraction but spent most of his life as a Protestant in England.
26. To alpinists, all mountains deserve respect and thus have a degree of holiness, but Kailash Parbat (Ganga Rinpoche to Tibetans) rates a special plug in Edwin Bernbaum's authoritative 1990 volume *Sacred Mountains of the World*, published by Random House (ISBN 0-87156-712-1).

In 2001, Reinhold Messner, one of the world's greatest current mountaineers, said of a proposed attempt to climb 6,638-meter Kailas Parbat: "If we conquer this mountain, then we conquer something in the soul of mankind. I suggest they go and climb something a little harder. Kailas is not so high and not so hard."

27. Sven Hedin, *Across the Gobi Desert* (New York: E. P. Dutton & Co., 1932), 363ff.
28. August Conrady (1864–1925), sinologist and scholar from Leipzig.
29. Founded prior to 1042 CE, this structure was pretty much wrecked in 1959 during the Chinese Cultural Revolution and assumption of control over Tibet. Fortunately, it had been extensively photographed for the British Museum in 1866.
30. Sven Hedin, *Trans-Himalaya: Discoveries and Adventures in Tibet*, vol. 3 (London: Macmillan & Co., 1913), 288.
31. The Sutlej rises in southwest Tibet and flows through the Himalayas to become one of the five rivers of the Punjab.

**Chapter III**

1. John Playfair (1748–1819), mathematician and geologist at the ancient and outstanding University of Edinburgh (founded in 1582), was (among other things) the first to attribute the transport of erratic boulders to glaciation. Playfair was also true to his name, for, in many of his publications, he reinforces (with bounteous credit) the theories advanced by his own predecessor, James Hutton (1726–1797), as in the latter's 1795 primer on geology, *Theory of the Earth*. Incidentally, Playfair's grandson, Henry (1789–1857), was the architect of the present university campus.
2. The year Forbes's book was published, 1843, was also the year in which James Prescott Joule determined the amount of work required to produce a given unit of heat.
3. Virgil is the ancient sage who also told us, "*Felix qui potuit rerum cognoscere causas Atque metus omnes*" — Happy is the man who is able to know the causes of things.
4. Protogene was a term once applied to rocks then deemed to be the oldest known on Earth. More stringent chemical analysis has since determined this constituent igneous mineral to be chlorite, rather than talc.
5. Innocent Le Masson, *Vie de Messire Jean d'Aranthon d'Alex, Éveque et Prince de Genéve* [Life of Sir John Aranthon Ales, Bishop and Prince of Geneva] (Lyon: Thibaud-Landriot, 1834).
6. Sir Andrew (1814–1891), a widely respected geomorphologist, succeeded Sir Roderick Impey Murchison (1792–1871), *the* authority on the Silurian Age, as head of the Geological Survey of Great Britain. This article was followed in 1860 by a full-length book bearing the same title.
7. Swift (1667–1745), a noted satirist of Anglo-Irish extraction, published his *Modest Proposal* in 1726 (wherein he suggested that any of the starving Irish could eat some of their numerous children). His better-known *Gulliver's Travels* came out in 1729, in the third section of which he described the inhabitants of the Island of Laputa who were all astronomers and other savants, sufficiently advanced and erudite that they could move their 10,000-acre island about, in, or above the ocean largely at will.
8. The glacier was not named not for the Alaskan "glacier priest," geologist and author Bernard Rosecrans Hubbard, SJ (1888–1962), but for the first president of the National Geographic Society, Gardiner Greene Hubbard (1822–1897).

**Chapter IV**

1. Kennedy (1817–1898) was cited by one of his peers, C. E. Mathews, in his obituary [*Alpine Journal,* Vol. XIX–155], as "The father of the Alpine Club, and no father ever regarded his offspring with a deeper or more lasting affection."
2. In *Alpine Journal,* Vol., XVIII, page 522ff, Charles Marret even published a historical critique of hotel services and prices throughout the Alps.
3. Dr. Maynard Malcolm Miller, glaciologist, mountaineer, legislator, and founder of the Juneau Icefield Research Project, has (in private communications to this scribe), indicated that palm trees were growing in coastal Alaska at about this same time.
4. "Illecillewaet" is the Okanagan Indian word for "rushing water," originally applied to the river flowing west from the glacier into the Columbia.
5. In 1982, the American Alpine Club published a quarto volume entitled *The Great Glacier and Its House* (ISBN 0-930410-13-0) in regard to this area.
6. An early, though not a founding, member of the Alpine Club, Tuckett (1834–1913) was a frequent contributor to its Journal.
7. This refers to the old church in the main yard of which Rev. W. A. B. Coolidge is buried.
8. Stated elsewhere (but not authoritatively) to be the daughter of the apostle St. Peter.
9. Much of the gold used by the Papacy and medieval European monarchs was derived from mines in the vast schistose formations of the Monte Rosa area.
10. This brief war of 1712 was settled by the Treaty of Aarau, by which each Swiss canton gained the right of religious self-determination; this soon led to nationwide freedom of religion.
11. Albert Heim (1849–1937), a noted Swiss geologist (and editor of the three-volume classic, *Geology of Switzerland*, 1905) was elected an honorary member of the Alpine Club in 1897.
12. One can still hear similar illogic, now expounded by equally uneducated American politicians, nearly two centuries later.
13. Elected a member of the Alpine Club in 1874, Eccles (1838–1915) was especially noted for his mastery of the summits near Mont Blanc. He often climbed with the popular Chamonix guide, Michel Payott (1840–1922).
14. Conway (1856–1937) was an arctic authority of great stature; Bonney (1833–1923) was a noted geologist specializing in Alpine stratigraphy.
15. Bill Field came by his respectable status quite honestly; members of the Field family had been prominent in various aspects of American society ever since Darby, a ferry operator of southern New Hampshire, had made the first ascent of Mount Washington in 1642.
16. This is also the latitude of Cape Muzon, subsequently agreed by all parties as the southern limit of Russian territory and the 1867 Alaska Purchase.
17. Mrs. Workman (1859–1925) was the patrician daughter of Massachusetts Governor Alexander Hamilton Bullock (1816–1882) of Worcester; Dr. Workman (1839–1918) was a retired, well-to-do medical doctor.
18. Fanny Bullock and William Hunter Workwan, *Two Summers in the Ice Wilds of Easter Karakoram* (New York: E. P. Dutton & Company, 1916) 217.

**Chapter V**

1. John Churchill was the tenth generation ancestor of another great English hero, Winston Leonard Spencer Churchill (1874–1965), who "The Mighty Duke of Marlbough at Blenheim won the day – And Oudenarde and Ramillies and Malplaquet" (Farjeons, *Heroes and Heroines* [New York: E. P. Dutton & Company, 1933].
2. There is considerable historical evidence that, while in the minority, all religions cry for freedom of conscience, but when they finally arrive in a position of control, their practitioners change their cry to one of calling for conformity of faith.
3. This act was reinforced by Pope John Paul II in 1992 when he formally forgave Galileo for any purported transgressions against ecclesiastical authority.
4. In 1774 the Papacy established its own astronomical research facility, the Specola Vaticana, near St. Peter's, and a century later, the great Pope Leo XIII relocated it to Castel Gandolfo because of light pollution in Rome. In 1961 it was further relocated to Mount Graham in Arizona, where further light pollution is becoming a major issue. But there is no suitable place on Earth for this observatory to flee to next.
5. Ben Nevis, the Zugspitze, Mount Fuji, the Pic du Midi, the Brocken, and Monte Cimone were among the other summits occupied, along with Mount Washington, of which only the first is now vacant.
6. The Signal Service was the bureaucratic creature of General William Babcock Hazen (1830–1887) and his successor, the Arctic hero General Adolphus Washington Greely (1844–1935). Much more on these folk and mountaintop observatory operations can be found in the 1991 publication *The Worst Weather on Earth* (ISBN 930410-35-1).
7. Budget cuts made under the Democratic administration of (Stephen) Grover Cleveland.
8. O'Keeffe's predecessor had also been discharged because of his frequent attacks of delirium tremens.
9. Rotch and Lowell shared a grandfather who was the noted industrialist and statesman, Abbott Lawrence (1792–1855), endower of Harvard's Lawrence Scientific School.
10. Afficionados of the rock glacier in King Ravine on the north side of Mount Madison, of which the "motion" is ice driven, might take some issue with this statement.

**Chapter VI**

1. The Holy See, supported by the annual "Peter's pence" sent to Rome from Gardar (at its peak), amounted to a value of 26.5 Norwegian marks and was paid in walrus ivory and hides, then liquidated at Bergen into silver, according to sources unearthed for us by Jan Bønding, Treasurer of the Danish Alpine Club. By the year 1500, after the Greenland colony had collapsed, the Norwegian mark had a value of 230 grams of silver.
2. Norse Christians used the disparaging word "skraeling," which translates as "wretched," to describe the non-Christian natives with whom they came into unfriendly contact in Greenland, Vinland, and Markland. The Norse application of their European farming values and subsistence customs to the Arctic and refusal to adopt any part of the natives' lifestyle was a major factor in the gradual deterioration

of the Norse colony. However, it was the Icelandic-American Vilhjalmur Stefansson (1879–1962) who later led the wider understanding that "going native" was the only sure way to survive in the Arctic.

3. The impressive remains of this structure can be seen in many modern tourist brochures.
4. The Pope did not actually specify a line "west of Greenwich" that would have dignified a burgeoning Protestant "fact." Instead, he stated it to be the meridian line "100 leagues west" of the Canary Islands. However, it remains clear that he believed the Earth to be a sphere.
5. These strategists included King Gustavus II Adolphus (regnant 1611–1632) and Count Axel Gustafsson Oxenstierna (1583–1654).
6. This event and its impact on human history, and several other comparable actions, have been analyzed in considerable detail in a series of articles in the *Bulletin of the American Meteorological Society*, written by Jehuda Neumann of the Hebrew University and her various collaborators.
7. The multitalented scientist James Richard Arnold (1923–2012) of UCLA was an important collaborator in this work.
8. *The Sun, the Earth, and Near-earth Space: A Guide to the Sun-Earth System,* compiled and published by NASA, 2009.
9. This sad event ended as a political decision made during the administration of President Richard M. Nixon and protested, loudly but vainly, by all manner of scientists, a good number of whom — like this scribe — thereby ended up on the presidential "enemies list."
10. This scribe once uncovered (from 10 feet below a moraine) a series of eastward-pointing glacial striations on the bedrock limestone crest of an unnamed, 10,000-foot-high peak in the now drier frontal range of the Canadian Rockies.
11. Records of the Hudson's Bay Company show that, over the past four centuries, their original posts at Moose Factory and Fort Churchill are now several hundred feet inland from tidewater, as Hudson's Bay has risen isostatically.
12. Mammoth bones can be safely dated by carbon$_{10}$ and have been found in association with human remains in various places in the southwestern United States. Furthermore, it appears that the first Americans may have eaten all the early horses (*eohippus*) that came east with them from the Old World. *Equus equus* was a much later Spanish import from Europe.
13. These various invaders of Alaska via the land bridge from Siberia to Alaska were able to reach the more temperate regions of the Americas by means of a relatively dry, ice-free corridor between the west edge of the Hudson's Bay Ice Sheet and the east edge of that which covered the Canadian Rockies.
14. The East Indies are presently a very active area, tectonically speaking, and land bridges have come and gone in the Tertiary era with a frequency unrelated to glacial epochs.
15. Following the line presently taken by Interstate Highway 15.
16. This number is not a typo but the result of another of Dr. Washburn's exercises in precision surveying. Recent research has determined that the high points of New Hampshire's Presidential Range may have occasionally been nunataks, projecting above the surface of the continental ice sheet.

17. In 1948, Dr. Bryan (1888–1950) advised this scribe that he should not waste time in mountaineering, saying, "Brad Washburn could have been a great geologist if he hadn't gotten involved with that sort of thing." A few years later, Harvard University gave Washburn, a mountaineer of enormous distinction and the longtime director of Boston's famed Museum of Science, an honorary doctorate in geology.

    Bryan's father, Richard William Dickinson Bryan (1849–1913), was astronomer and chaplain of the ill-fated American polar expedition of 1871, commanded by Charles Francis Hall (1821–1871), who was poisoned by members of his discontented crew.
18. "Caliche" is a Spanish term applied to soil that has been partially solidified by the infusion of sodium nitrate or calcium carbonate.

**Chapter VII**

1. No two of the Sun's eight or nine planets are alike in size, composition, or position, but the rotational axis of Uranus is flat on its side and unique in being almost exactly in the plane of its orbit.
2. From the thirteenth century to the end of the Great War, Austria had a saltwater port at Trieste, complete with navy. Austria-Hungary was also a major player in the nineteenth century (and pre-Great War) international game of scientific and polar exploration.
3. As well, the members of Lieutenant Greely's Lady Franklin Bay Expedition of 1881–1884 kept happily warm at their post of Fort Conger by burning the coal found extensively on Ellesmere Island.
4. Earth's Moon contributes its own regular nineteen-year cycle of rotational position in its revolutions around its parent.
5. Contributing to the sea floor clutter, the amount of British merchant tonnage sunk by German U-boats during but one month in the autumn of 1941 totaled in excess of 300,000 tons.
6. J. D. Hays, John Imbrie, and N. J. Shackleton, "Variations in the Earth's Orbit: Pacemaker of the Ice Ages," *Science* 194, no. 4270 (10 December 1976): 1121–1132.
7. The subtitle was "For 500,000 years, major climatic changes have followed variations in obliquity and precession."
8. "Anthropogenic" is a 98-cent word. According to the Oxford English Dictionary, 2000 (Vol. I; p. 511), "Having its origin in the activities of man."

**Chapter VIII**

1. "The truth shall set you free." Johns Hopkins (1795–1873) was a self-made, Maryland-born businessman, financier, and philanthropist who left $7,000,000 to jointly support a hospital and a university.
2. Jean-Baptiste-Pierre-Antoine de Monet de Lamarck (1744–1829). He originated Lamarckianism. He was a distinguished French medical doctor and naturalist who predated Charles Darwin by half a century in his research and publications.
3. This remark is made in regard to the legal tribulations of John Thomas Scopes (1900–1970), a high school teacher who taught evolution in defiance of a Tennessee

state law (which was later repealed), which was very much in the news at the time this article was written.

4. Samuel Wilberforce (1805–1873) was a noted Anglican prelate whose oratorical facility was apparently greater than his factual learning. His father, William (1759–1833), was far more outstanding — as a humanitarian.
5. Johann Frederick Blumenbach (1752–1840), professor of medicine at Göttingen, was a pioneer in the study of man as a species.
6. Jean-Etienne Guettard (1715–1786) completed the first geological map of France in 1777.
7. Smith was a civil engineer who designed canals and became the unintentional founder of stratigraphical geology. His publication in 1815 of *A Delineation of the Strata of England and Wales* started the process of getting Earth history in order.
8. The first serious critique disputing Ussher's chronology was written by an Irish Catholic priest, Father John MacEnery (1797–1841), who had also studied fossil remnants found in the caves of south England.
9. This town at the south end of the Lake of Pfäffikon, east of Zurich, is well known for the findings of a Bronze Age civilization among the lake dwellers of this area.
10. Named for a village in upper Austria, which is the site of an early Iron Age culture, of about 900 BCE, that shows the development of art objects.
11. Marble is an altered form of limestone, calcium carbononate ($CaCO_3$), and reacts to the sulfur dioxide that is a major constituent of most smog and acid rain by turning black and crumbling.
12. Since the Christian missionaries who accompanied (and followed) Francisco Pizarro González (1471–1541) were savagely successful in destroying every element of the pagan culture of Atahualpa's Incas, it has been impossible to determine if the ancestors of these folk lived high in the mountains voluntarily or were driven away from the more fertile valleys by the invaders after 1533.
13. Some of the modern Jewish dietary rules have a similar derivation, evolved from the practicalities of living in a desert area.
14. Some climbing expeditions in the Karakoram (1,000 miles from Mount Everest) have used native Balti for help in high-altitude ascents but found that they did not compare in effectiveness to the Sherpas.

**Chapter IX**

1. Armageddon is known as the hill of Megiddo in some writings. But we are not concerned here with the immediate text of the pertinent passage in the Book of Revelations (16:16) so much as with its symbolism as the cataclysmic event of mankind, when all civilized restraints are ignored in the raw, primitive, desperate, and (ultimately) futile search for sheer personal survival.
2. The so-called Communist Chinese leadership has met this issue with forthright vigor, for which their reward has been to receive frequent abuse from the "more enlightened" leaders of so-called Christian nations. Regrettably, they have not shown similar courage in dealing with environmental issues.
3. Jared Diamond, *Collapse: How Societies Choose to Fail or Succeed*, rev. ed. (New York: Penguin, 2011).

4. Mankind cannot take our current lifestyle and flee to any of the Sun's other planets; not one of them is even slightly receptive to our needs. We could consider going somewhere else in our galaxy, such as Alpha Centauri, but it is a very, very long trip, and it will require a lot of fossil fuel, travel time, and food just to get there. Who among us is up to surviving such a trip? And at this time, we don't have a clue as to what we might find if we did get to that nearest star cluster.
5. Dr. G. Wesley Lockwood had in mind "about thirty years," whereas a recent climatological study states it more precisely — at the year 2047.

**Appendix of Comparisons**

1. More famously associated with the Risorgimento movement were Victor Emmanuel II (1820–1878), previously ruler of Sardinia/Savoy, who became King of Italy in 1861; Giuseppe Garibaldi (1807–1882), a soldier of fortune who led the Cacciatori delle Alpi; and Camillo Benso, Count of Cavour (1810–1861), who masterminded the international politics of the effort while the senior Sella handled the negotiations within the Italian peninsula for this quasi-military effort.
2. Much of recent European history, as well as that of the world, would likely have been different if the Duke had occupied the throne of Italy instead of his much weaker cousin, Victor Emmanuel III. The Duke (commander of the Italian Navy in much of the Great War) was a man of formidable ambition coupled with very good judgment.
3. The forty-five-year-old Ötsi, possibly a trader or shaman, was apparently crossing the Schnalstal Glacier some 5,300 years in the past and met with foul play while so doing.

*Der Muth der Wahrheit ist die erste Bedingung des philosophischen Studiums.*

*The courage of truth is the first qualification for philosophic studies.*

— Georg Wilhelm Friedrich Hegel (1770–1831)

Hills of Ireland

# Index

My aim and desire is to see how the words and phrases lie in the holy text, and to discern somewhat of the same, for my own contente.

— Wm. Bradford, Puritan; 1652

# About the Author

Bill Putnam was born in Springfield, Massachusetts, on October 25, 1924, the third of six children born to Roger and Caroline Putnam. While studying geology at Harvard, he volunteered to fight in World War II, enlisting as a private and joining the elite 10th Mountain Division, a specialized ski unit trained to fight in mountainous and arctic conditions. He served in both the Aleutian and Italian campaigns, rising to the rank of first lieutenant along the way. During a skirmish near Castel d'Aiano in the Apennine Mountains of Italy, Putnam was wounded, picking up some shrapnel that remains in his body today. The resulting injury earned him a Purple Heart but didn't keep him out of action for long. He was later decorated for gallantry in action, earning both the Silver and Bronze Stars.

After the war ended, Putnam went back to Harvard and finished his schooling in geology. He then landed a job in the geology department at Tufts University as the "third person in a two-person department," as he would later recall.

By 1952, Putnam was back in Springfield, working at the Greater Springfield Chamber of Commerce. This job didn't last long, as he soon turned his attention to television, founding in 1953 WWLP, Springfield's first TV station and the first licensed UHF television station in the United States. Here, he met and worked with future TV personality Kitty Broman, whom he later married. His Springfield Television Corporation would later buy four more stations before he sold the company and retired from the business in 1984. In addition to many other broadcasting honors, Putnam was inducted into the Broadcasting Hall of Fame in 2001.

While making a name for himself in the broadcasting world, Putnam also became prominent in alpinist circles. He made several first ascents and exploratory expeditions in the Selkirk Mountains of British Columbia, establishing himself as a distinguished American climber. He served as president of the American Alpine Club and vice president and council member of the International Mountaineering and Climbing Federation (UIAA). He also was the U.S. delegate to the UIAA for thirty years. In 2002, an alpine hut in the Selkirk Mountains was renamed the Bill Putnam Hut in his honor.

After retiring from broadcasting, Bill Putnam accepted a new challenge, one that he took very seriously and into which he put all of his energy and resources. His brother Michael was ready to step down as sole trustee of Lowell Observatory, and Bill gladly jumped into this position that he would hold for twenty-six years until retiring in 2013. During his tenure as sole trustee, Bill led efforts to build the Steele Visitor Center in 1994, the Discovery Channel Telescope in 2012, and the Putnam Collection Center, named in honor of him and his family in 2014.

Light Technology PUBLISHING Presents

eBook Available on Amazon, Apple iTunes, Google Play, and Barnes & Noble

ISBN: 978-0-930410-50-6
eISBN: 978-1-62233-694-4

# GREEN COGNAC

## The Education of a Mountain Fighter

by William Lowell Putnam III

In early 1943, William Lowell Putnam III joined what was to become the 10th Mountain Division, the first and only mountain warfare unit of the U.S. Army. *Green Cognac: The Education of a Mountain Fighter* is a superb account of the mountain and ski troops as seen from Putnam's often wry perspective.

The story of what transpired during the brief, eventful years of war is told by one who was well acquainted with the mountains and mountaineering before he became a mountain fighter. Putnam applied this knowledge while serving in the infantry regiments of the 10th Mountain Division. The elite mountain troops were sent to break the German Gothic Line in the Apennine Mountains of Italy. Brilliantly led, they fought their way northward with magnificent dash, seizing control of ten mountain crests. Their determined drive broke the German resistance and brought on the first large-scale enemy surrender of World War II.

Much celebrated and studied after the war for their striking success and spirit in the field, the mountain troops presented an awe-inspiring picture of camaraderie and courage. From the bold ski-trooper concept, first suggested in 1940, to the final days of demobilization at the end of 1945, this is their story.

Also Available in Print on Amazon.com

Light Technology PUBLISHING Presents

eBook Available on Amazon, Apple iTunes, Google Play, and Barnes & Noble

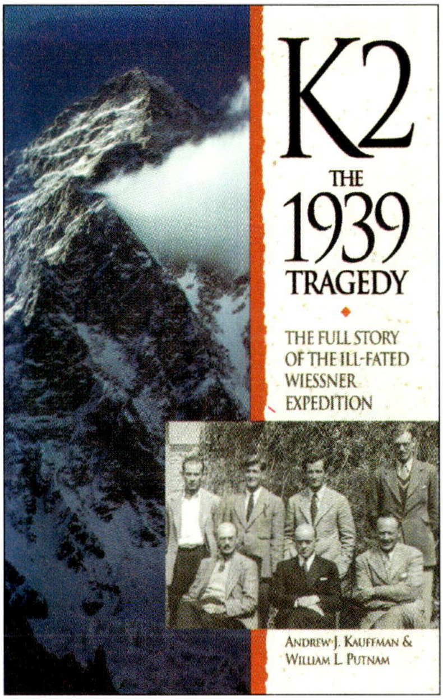


ISBN: 978-0-89886-323-9
eISBN: 978-1-62233-695-1

# K2 THE 1939 TRAGEDY

## The Full Story of the Ill-Fated Wiessner Expedition

by William Lowell Putnam III and Andrew J. Kauffman

The story of the 1939 American K2 expedition is well known among mountaineers: World-class German-born climber Fritz Wiessner and Pasang Dawa Lama came within 800 feet of attaining the world's second-highest unclimbed summit before turning back for more supplies. Rejoining them on the descent was Dudley Wolfe, who had stayed not far below. When reaching the lower camps, the party found them stripped of supplies and deserted. Wiessner decided to descend further to investigate, leaving Wolfe behind — alone.

Later, unable to descend solo, Wolfe had to be rescued; but the attempt failed, and Wolfe and Sherpas Pasang Kikuli, Pasang Kitar, and Phinsoo died. Initially, Wiessner was held responsible, but in time, the blame shifted to climber Jack Durrance and another sherpa. The disaster was considered one of the worst accidents in the climbing history of the Himalayas. It was also the subject of much speculation for years afterward; in 1961, Italian climber Fosco Maraini claimed it a tragedy "on which no full light has ever been shed."

For some historians, the speculation would not rest. There were too many missing pieces, inconsistencies, and unanswered questions for a disaster of this scale. Unfortunately, reliable documentation was scarce, and so was the cooperation of the remaining expedition members, who did not want to rekindle the controversy that arose from the expedition's failure. They echoed the neutral statement issued by the investigating committee of the American Alpine Club in 1940, which said, in effect, "let sleeping dogs lie."

Also Available in Print on Amazon.com

Light Technology PUBLISHING Presents

eBook Available on Amazon, Apple iTunes, Google Play, and Barnes & Noble

ISBN: 978-0-930410-35-3
eISBN: 978-1-62233-701-9

# The Worst Weather on Earth

## A History of the Mount Washington Observatory

by William Lowell Putnam III

"There may be worse weather, from time to time, at some forbidding place on planet Earth, but it has yet to be reliably recorded."

So begins *The Worst Weather on Earth: A History of the Mount Washington Observatory*. Mount Washington, at 6,288 feet above sea level, is one of the highest elevations in the eastern United States and is subject to some of the fiercest weather patterns in the world. Situated close to major centers of population, it has been an accessible objective for travelers. The curious, the intrepid, the scientific — Mount Washington has attracted them all.

In this age of satellites and advanced instrumentation, the intricacies of weather observation are now taken for granted. However, not so long ago, weather was a blank on the scientific map of understanding. *The Worst Weather on Earth* chronicles the social and scientific milieu of those who have recorded the weather on the mountain for over one hundred years.

Included are chapters such as "Radio on the Rockpile," which covers the pioneering days of radio broadcasting from the summit, and "Rime and Reason," which presents a fascinating discussion of rime and the problems of icing that were researched extensively on the summit.

*The Worst Weather on Earth* is rendered more immediate by the liberal use of contemporary accounts; excerpts from letters, reports, and the log notes of the summit observers abound, giving the flavor and the excitement of over a century of scientific observation and discovery.

Also Available in Print on Amazon.com

# Light Technology PUBLISHING Presents

eBooks Available on Amazon, Apple iTunes, Google Play, and Barnes & Noble

## ARCTIC SUPERSTARS

A CENTENNIAL PUBLICATION OF THE AMERICAN ALPINE CLUB

***The scientific exploration and study of high mountain elevations and of the regions lying within or about the Arctic and Antarctic Circles***

*by William Lowell Putnam III*

ISBN: 978-0-930410-82-7
eISBN: 978-1-62233-686-9

## A YANKEE IMAGE

THE LIFE AND TIMES OF ROGER LOWELL PUTNAM

*by William Lowell Putnam III*

ISBN: 978-0-914659-55-6
eISBN 978-1-62233-697-5

## THE KAISER'S MERCHANT SHIPS IN WORLD WAR I

*by William Lowell Putnam III*

ISBN: 978-0-7864-0923-5
eISBN: 978-1-62233-699-9

Also Available in Print on Amazon.com

# Light Technology PUBLISHING Presents

eBooks Available on Amazon, Apple iTunes, Google Play, and Barnes & Noble

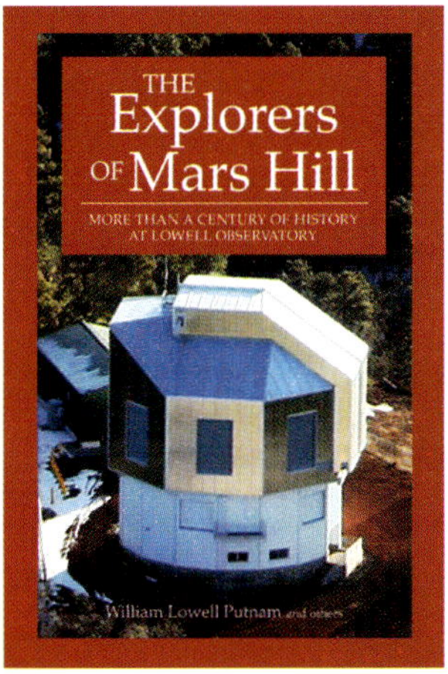


## The Explorers of Mars Hill

MORE THAN A CENTURY OF HISTORY AT LOWELL OBSERVATORY

*by William Lowell Putnam III*

ISBN: 978-0-914659-69-3
eISBN: 978-1-62233-679-1

## Percival Lowell's BigRed Car

THE TALE OF AN ASTRONOMER AND A 1911 STEVENS-DURYEA

*by William Lowell Putnam III*

ISBN: 978-0-7864-1234-1
eISBN: 978-1-62233-698-2

## The Education of an Alpinist

TALES OF A GRANDFATHER

*by William Lowell Putnam III*

eISBN: 978-1-62233-693-7

## Joe Dodge

ONE NEW HAMPSHIRE INSTITUTION

*by William Lowell Putnam III*

ISBN: 978-0-914659-17-4
eISBN: 978-1-62233-691-3

Also Available in Print on Amazon.com

# Light Technology PUBLISHING Presents

eBooks Available on Amazon, Apple iTunes, Google Play, and Barnes & Noble

## John Peter Zenger and the Fundamental Freedom

*by William Lowell Putnam III*

ISBN: 978-0-7864-0370-7
eISBN: 978-1-62233-700-2

## Place Names of the Canadian Alps

*by William Lowell Putnam III, Glen W. Boles, Roger W. Laurilla*

ISBN: 978-0-9691621-4-8
eISBN: 978-1-62233-702-6

## The Great Glacier and Its House The Story of the First Alpinism in North America 1885-1925

*by William Lowell Putnam III*

ISBN: 978-0-930410-13-1
eISBN: 978-1-62233-688-3

## The Guiding Spirit

*by William Lowell Putnam III and Andrew J. Kauffman*

ISBN: 978-0-9691621-2-4
eISBN: 978-1-62233-692-0

Also Available in Print on Amazon.com

# *Other Books by William Lowell Putnam*

HOW WE SURVIVED IN UHF TELEVISION
A BROADCASTING MEMOIR, 1953-1984
*by Kitty Broman Putnam and William Lowell Putnam III*

ISBN: 978-0-7864-6666-5
eISBN: 978-1-62233-696-8
eBook Available on Amazon, Apple iTunes, Google Play, and Barnes & Noble

TORQUEMADA REVISITED
THE POWER OF EFFECTIVE PERSUASION ON INTELLECTUAL FREEDOM AND RACISM
*by William Lowell Putnam III*

eISBN: 978-1-62233-704-0
eBook Available on Amazon and Apple iTunes

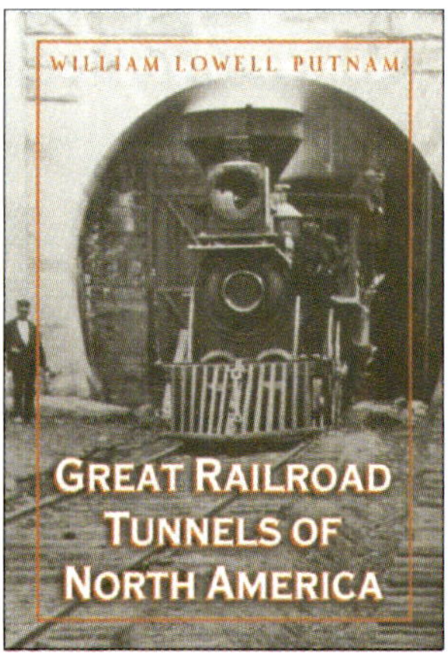


GREAT RAILROAD TUNNELS OF NORTH AMERICA
*by William Lowell Putnam III*

ISBN: 978-0-7864-5951-3
eBook Available on Amazon and Google Play

A CENTURY OF AMERICAN ALPINISM 2002
*by Fay, Bent, Palmer, Thorington, Kauffman, Putnam*

ASIN: B000HYTN20
Only Available in Print